ONE - STOP ENGLISH

- English Revolution in 3 Months -

ONE - STOP ENGLISH

ONE - STOP ENGLISH

- English Revolution in 3 Months -

초판 1쇄 펴낸 날 · 2007년 6월 1일 | **초판 3쇄 펴낸 날** · 2014년 5월 26일
지은이 · 박규일 | **펴낸이** · 원성삼
등록번호 · 제2-1349호(1992. 3. 31) | **펴낸 곳** · 예영커뮤니케이션
주소 · (136-825) 서울시 성북구 성북로 6가길 31 | **홈페이지** www.jeyoung.com
출판사업부 · T. (02)766-8931 F. (02)766-8934 e-mail : jeyoung@chol.com
출판유통사업부 · T. (02)766-7912 F. (02)766-8934 e-mail : jeyoung@chol.com

Copyright ⓒ 2007, 박규일

ISBN 978-89-8350-711-2 (03740)

값 12,000원

ONE - STOP ENGLISH

- English Revolution in 3 Months -

박규일 지음

예영커뮤니케이션

"만남이 우리의 인생을 좌우한다."는 평범한 진리를 우리는 잘 알고 있습니다. 아이들은 친구를, 학생은 선생님을, 회사원은 사장님을, 사업가는 파트너를, 부부는 배우자를 서로 잘 만나야 한다고 합니다. 좋은 만남은 인생을 풍요롭게 만들고 가치 있게 만듭니다. 반면에 잘못된 만남은 인생을 거칠게 만들고 황폐화시킵니다.

당신이 ONE STOP ENGLISH를 선택한다면 그것은 탁월한 선택이 될 것입니다.

오늘 당신과 ONE STOP ENGLISH와의 만남은 최고의 만남이 될 것입니다. 당신이 ONE STOP ENGLISH를 선택한다면 그것은 탁월한 선택이 될 것입니다. 특별히 가슴에 영어의 한을 가지고 평생을 살아오신 분들에게 이 책을 추천합니다. ONE STOP ENGLISH는 영어가 안 된다고 생각하시는 분, 영어의 실패자라고 생각하시는 분, 이제 막 영어에 입문하시는 분, 수능고사나 토익·토플 시험을 준비하시는 분, 단기간에 영어의 문법 체계를 정립시키고 싶은 분들에게 최고의 선물이 될 것입니다.

ONE STOP ENGLISH가 세상에 나온 데에는 두 가지 목적이 있습니다. 첫째, 대한민국 국민 모두가 단기간의 학습 과정을 통해서 영어의 자신감을 회복하고 글로벌 리더가 되게 하는 데 있습니다. 지금과 같이 국가 간의 장벽이 허물어지고 국제교류가 활성화되는데 비해 한국인의 영어 커뮤니케이션 능력의 저하는 국제적인 조롱을 받기까지 했습니다. 이제 우리는 이러한 현실을 뛰어넘어 국제 사회를 이끌어가야 합니다. 한국과 같이 국토가 비좁고 인구가 많은 상황에서는 많은 인구의 국제 사회로의 진출이 절실히 필요합니다. 지난 9년 동안 OMS(ONE STOP ENGLISH Miracle System)은 전국에 수많은 사람들을 영어의 지름길로 안내해 왔습니다. 그 사례는 헤아릴 수가 없습니다. 2006년 12월에는 세계 최초로 영어학습법 특허출원(출원번호 10-2006-137708호)이 되었습니다. 이제는 명실 공히 국내 최고의 영어 단기 완성 프로그램으로 인정을 받게 되었습니다. ONE STOP ENGLISH는 이러한 공신력 있는 교육 효과를 바탕으로 당신에게 글로벌 리더의 길을 열어줄 것입니다.

둘째, 그리스도인들이 영어성경을 정확하게 해석하고 이해하게 하여 세계 선교에 앞장서도록 하기 위해서입니다. 이미 잘 알려진 것처럼 성경은 세계 최고의 베스트셀러입니다. 그리고 영어성경은 최고의 영어 교과서입니다. 영어성경이 최고의 가치가 있는 이유는 영어성경이 독일어에서 영어로 번역될 때, 당대 최고의 학자들에 의해 번역이 되었기 때문입니다. 그러므로 영어문장 하나하나가 세련되고, 수준 높은 고급문장으로 구성되어 있습니다. 또한 영어성경은 다양한 문학 장르를 포함하고 있습니다. 이야기 형식, 논설 형식, 시문학 형식 등 여러 형식의 문장을 대할 수 있습니다. 특별히 영어성경은 하나님의 감동으로 기록된 책으로 수많은 교훈이 담겨져 있기 때문에 성경을 읽는 독자에게 큰 감동과 지혜를 전달합니다. OMS선교훈련원에서는 영어성경 공부교재를 지속적으로 제작 보급하여 진리와 영어에 목말라하는 모든 분들에게 생수가 될 것입니다.

ONE STOP ENGLISH가 세상에 나오기까지 우리 주 하나님의 특별한 사랑과 은혜가 있었습니다. 여러 번의 시련이 있었고 그때마다 나약해져

가는 마음을 우리 주 하나님은 강하게 하셨습니다.

또 한 분에게 감사드립니다. 무명인의 원고를 기꺼이 받아주시고 책으로 세상에 나올 수 있도록 도와주신 예영커뮤니케이션 김승태 대표님에게 감사드립니다. 대표님은 저에게 꿈을 이루도록 도와주신 진정한 Dream Builder가 되어 주셨습니다. 책의 완성도를 높이기 위해 애써 주신 OMS 선교훈련원에 여러 선생님에게 감사드립니다. 특별히 마지막 손질까지 바쁜 시간을 쪼개어 교정을 봐 주신 OMS선교훈련원 박혜영 교수부장님에게 감사드립니다. 부족한 아들을 위해 새벽마다 기도해 주신 나의 어머니 채만심 권사님, 장모 오미숙 집사님에게 사랑의 빚을 졌습니다. 지금은 천국에 계신 장인 이동기 안수집사님은 저에게 언제나 든든한 후원자였습니다. 그 외에 일일이 이름을 나열할 수는 없지만 ONE STOP ENGLISH를 사랑해 주신 많은 분들에게 감사드립니다. 마지막으로 오랜 시간 관심과 사랑, 인내로 기도하며 기다려 준 나의 아내 이두연, 그리고 사랑하는 아들 영진, 세진과 기쁨을 나누고 싶습니다.

2007년 3월 16일
방배동 연구실에서 박 규일

가장 빨리, 가장 정확하게, 가장 쉽게 영어를 정복하는 지름길

 영어는 외국어이지만 우리에 모국어만큼 중요한 언어로 부상하고 있다. 영어의 광풍은 조기유학으로 이어지고 여름 방학이면 인천 국제공항이 어학연수 학생들로 북새통을 이룬다. 그렇게 공부한 영어가 막상 투자에 비해 성과는 미미하다. 나 역시 대학교에서 어학원을 맡아 여러 프로그램을 도입해 보았지만 만족스런 결과를 보지 못했다. 그러던 중 박규일 원장님의 강의를 접하게 되었고, 영어혁명이 과장이 아니라는 것을 알게 되었다. 모든 것에 지름길이 있듯이 영어에도 지름길이 있다는 말에 공감을 한다. 영어 설계도와 공식, 단어암기법, 해석공식, 영작공식이 하나의 톱니바퀴처럼 맞물려 돌아가면서 영어가 완성되어져 가는 것은 영어의 전 과정을 가장 빨리, 가장 정확하게, 가장 쉽게 영어를 정복하는 지름길이라 하겠다. 부디 많은 분들이 박규일 원장님이 저술한 「ONE STOP ENGLISH」를 통해 영어의 늪에서 빠져 나가기를 바란다.

정규훈 교수 / 총신대학교 어학원 원장(現)

영어 학습자의 필독서

「ONE STOP ENGLISH」는 영어를 공부하는 학생이라면 누구나 반드시 읽어야 할 필독서라 생각된다. 독자들이 본서를 손에 넣었다는 것은 큰 행운이다. 본서는 영어를 정복하는 데 필요한 가이드라인을 제시해 줄 것이고 영어에 대한 고민을 속 시원하게 해결해 줄 것이다. 차분하게 학습한다면 반드시 보물을 발견할 것이다.

김덕겸 교수 / 한영신학대학교 동시통역대학원(現)

*ONE STOP ENGLISH*는 영어의 끝을 보여 준다

대한민국 사람의 소원이 통일이 아니라 영어를 잘 하는 것이라 할 정도로 영어는 이제 한 국가의 경쟁력이 되었고 개인의 경쟁력이 되었다. 그 숙제를 해결하는 데 「ONE STOP ENGLISH」가 큰 기여를 하리라 믿는다. 특별히 내가 접한 「ONE STOP ENGLISH」는 어느 누구도 이야기 하지 않은 영어에 설계도를 이야기함으로 영어에 끝을 보여 주고 있는 것이 큰 특징이라 하겠다. 대한민국 국민으로 영어에 한을 가지고 살아가는 모두에게 본서를 적극 추천한다.

유충열 목사 / 터치 코리아 셀 크리닉 원장(現),한국교회 셀 전략 연구소 소장(現)

국제화 시대의 글로벌 리더

타문화권 선교의 사명을 감당하기 원하는 이들에게는 영적 자질과 더불어 많은 자연적 자질과 자격이 필요하다. 그 중에서도 가장 중요한 자질이 언어 능력이다. 커뮤니케이션을 영어로 수행하는 능력을 학습하기 위한 좋은 교재도 많이 나와 있지만 나름대로의 한계가 있는 것도 사실이다. 이번에 박일규 원장님이 영어에 관한 다년간의 관심과 전문성으로 「ONE STOP ENGLISH」를 출간하게 된 것은 참으로 반가운 일이다. 독특한 학습방법을 통해 영어로 성경을 읽고 영어로 복음을 전할 수 있는 능력을 단기간 내에 배양할 수 있다는 것은 참으로 의미 있는 일이라 하겠다. 본 교재는 우리 청소년들이 국제화 시대에 글로벌 리더로 자라나는 데 영어를 이해하고 학습함에 있어 새로운 통찰을 제공할 수 있을 것이라 확신한다.

김원경 / 코리아헤럴드 편집부 차장 (前) KBS 국제방송 작가(前)

Contents

약어표

주어(S) 공식 6가지 ‖ 동사(V) 공식 8가지 ‖ 목적어(O) 공식 7가지

목적어+보어(O+C) 공식 5가지 ‖ 보어(C) 공식 6가지 ‖ 형용사구(a.p) 공식 3가지

형용사절(a.c.) 공식 2가지 ‖ 부사구(ad.p) 공식 3가지 ‖ 부사절(ad.c) 공식 9가지

영어의 비밀이 풀렸다

1 UNIT

"한국 사람은 10년을 영어 공부해도 안 된다."는 말이 있다. 이 말은 중학교 3년, 고등학교 3년, 대학교 4년, 합해서 10년 동안 영어공부를 해도 외국인을 만나면 영어로 말 한마디 못하고, 영어로 자기소개문 하나 정도 자신 있게 쓰지 못하기 때문이다.

한국 사람들이 영어를 10년 이상 배워도 안 되는 이유

신학대학원을 졸업한 목회자 중에 영어성경을 정확하게 해석하는 목회자가 의외로 많지 않다. 무엇이 문제인가? 왜 영어정복이 어려운가? 지난 8년 동안 현장에서 ONE STOP ENGLISH를 가르치면서 가장 많이 받은 질문은 "나 같은 영어 왕초보도 정말 3개월이면 영어를 정복할 수 있습니까?"라는 말이었다. 그도 그럴 것이 영어 프로그램의 제목이 "3개월 영어 혁명"이었기 때문이다. 이런 질문을 받을 때마다 나는 언제나 주저하지 않고 분명하게 답을 해 준다.

"이번이야말로 당신이 영어의 한을 풀 수 있는 처음이자 마지막 기회일 수 있습니다. 영어는 정복할 수가 있습니다. 왜냐하면 지난 8년 동안 수많은 학생들이 ONE STOP ENGLISH를 들었고, 하루에 1시간 30분 정도의 시간을 매일 투자한 학생들은 한 사람도 실패하지 않았기 때문입니다."

방방곡곡에서 넘쳐
나는 ONE STOP
ENGLISH를 공부한
사람들의 성공담

그동안 ONE STOP ENGLISH를 공부한 사람들의 신나는 후일담을 나는 종종 듣는다. 영어공부를 접은 지 30년이나 지난 어느 40대 아버지가 3개월 만에 영어를 정복해 영자신문과 원서들을 정확하게 해석하고 고등학생 자녀를 손수 지도해서 영어성적을 수직 상승하게 한 이야기, 초등학교 6학년 학생이 학습 3개월 만에 수능문제를 완벽하게 풀어낸 이야기, 영어에 기초가 없었던 환갑을 바라보는 기업체 사장님이 3개월 만에 영어성경과 에세이를 스스로 해석하며 읽게 된 이야기, 평범한 중학교 학생이 3개월 만에 6,000개의 영단어를 암기한 이야기, 보통 실력의 중학교 1학년 학생이 3개월이 지나면서 고3 수능문제를 거의 완벽하게 풀어낸 이야기, 영어를 포기했던 목사님들이 3개월 만에 영어성경과 영어원서를 정확하게 해석한 이야기 등이다. ONE STOP ENGLISH를 통해 영어공부에 자신감을 갖게 된 경우는 헤아릴 수 없을 정도로 많다.

지금도 방배동 OMS영어훈련원을 비롯하여 전국의 여러 지역에서 펼쳐지고 있는 OMS영어교육을 통해 영어정복의 꿈같은 이야기들이 넘쳐나고 있다. 무엇이 3개월 영어혁명을 가능케 했는가? 여기에는 분명한 이유가 있다.

영어를 정복하려면
영어의 구조와 특징을
알아야 한다.

손자병법에 "지피지기면 백전백승"(知彼知己 百戰百勝)이라는 말이 있다. 이 말은 "적을 알고 나를 알면 백전백승이다"라는 뜻이다. 정말 맞는 말이다. 마찬가지로 먼저 영어라는 적을 이기기 위해서는 내가 속한 나랏말인 한글의 구조와 특징을 알아야 한다. 그리고 영어의 구조와 특징을 알아야 한다. 그렇게 되면 분명 한글과 영어의 차이점을 발견할 수 있게 되고 그 차이를 극복하면 자연스럽게 영어의 해법을 발견할 수 있게 될 것이다. 나는 한국인들이 오랫동안 영어공부를 하려고 노력했음에도 불구하고 왜 자신감을 잃는지 의문을 풀어가다가 자연스럽게 습성화된 언어의 구조 차이에서 비롯된다는 것을 깨달았다. 그리고 기나긴 연구를 통해 영어학습의 실마리를 찾았다. 이것이 3개월 영어혁명이 성공하는 이유이다.

그렇다면 우리말에는 어떤 특징을 가지고 있을까? 영어를 한 마디로 정의한다면 영어는 각자의 자리가 있다고 해서 '자리언어'(Position Language)라고 정의 할 수 있다.

영어는 자리의 언어이다.

누구나 학창 시절에 운동장에서 조회를 한 경험이 있을 것이다. 운동장에서 반듯하게 줄을 서려고 할 때, 가장 중요한 것이 있다. 그것이 있어야 우리가 줄을 설 수 있다. 무엇일까?

기준이다. 기준이 없이는 위치를 잡을 수 없고 자리를 잡을 수 없다. 기준의 조건이 있다면 무엇인가?

첫 번째, 자리를 잡으려고 할 때 반드시 나와야 한다. 두 번째, 다른 사람은 다 움직여도 기준 만큼은 절대 움직이면 안 된다. 그 자리에 서 있어야 한다. 이것이 바로 기준의 두 가지 조건이다. 위치를 잡거나 줄을 서려고 할 때 반드시 필요한 것이 바로 '기준'이다. 영어는 자리언어이기 때문에 기준이 필요하다.

자리언어인 영어의 기준이 무엇인가? 우리가 영어문장을 쓰거나 또는 영어문장을 읽으려고 할 때 반드시 나오는 것이 있다. 무엇인가? 바로 주어와 동사이다. 또 한 가지, 언제나 주어는 동사 앞에 나와야 하고 동사는 주어 뒤에 나온다. 언제나 그 자리에 나오기 때문에 기준의 조건이 된다. 자리언어인 영어의 기준은 주어와 동사이다.

다시 추억 속으로 돌아가 보자. 옛날에 중학교에 처음 들어갔을 때 배웠던 문장 중에서 혹시 기억나는 문장 있는가? "I am a boy."라는 문장이 있었다. 기억나는가? "나는 소년이다."라는 아주 간단한 문장이다.

이 문장의 패턴 S+V+★이다.

중학교 1학년의 영어문장은 주어, 동사, 보어 이렇게 아주 간단하게 구성되어 있다. 중요한 것은 학년이 올라갈수록 문장의 구조가 바뀐다는 것이다. 어떻게 바뀌는가? 영어의 기준인 주어와 동사를 기준으로 보면 아래와 같다.

```
주어+동사+★
중1~2       --S---V-----.
중3~고1     ----S---V--------
고2~3학년 -------S---V----------
토플·토익   -----------S------V-----------------
```

문장이 길어지고 복문으로 되면 어느 단어가 주어인지 동사인지 구분이 안 된다.

중학교 1학년 문장은 어렵지 않았다. "I am a boy."를 배울 때만 해도 영어는 쉬운 과목이었고, 누구나 해볼 만한 과목이라고 생각했다. 그런데 어느 순간에 보니까 영어공부에 대한 자신감을 잃고 어려운 과목이 되어 버렸다. 심지어는 포기까지 했다.

왜 영어공부에 실패했을까? 학년이 올라갈수록 문장 구조가 막 바뀌는데 학생들이 그 바뀌는 패턴에 적응하지 못했기 때문이다. "I am a boy."를 배우던 중학교 1학년 때, 미리 영어 문장에는 "I am a boy." 수준의 문장만 있는 것이 아니라 주어와 동사를 기준으로 영어문장의 변화 구조를

처음 배울 때는 간단한 문장 구조가 학년이 올라갈수록 문장의 구조가 바뀐다.

미리 알았더라면 영어정복의 길이 쉽게 열렸을 것이다.

........................S.........................V........................

영어의 모든 문장은 주어와 동사를 중심으로 3개의 자리로 구분된다.

주어의 앞자리 (A)

주어와 동사 사이 자리(B)

동사 다음 자리.(C)

Ⓐ+주어(S)+Ⓑ+동사(V)+Ⓒ

주어 앞자리(A)는 **부사, 부사구, 형용사구, 부사절**

주어와 동사 사이 자리(B)는 **형용사, 형용사구, 형용사절, 부사**

동사 다음의 자리(C)는 **목적어, 보어, 형용사 ,형용사구, 형용사절, 부사, 부사구, 부사절**

이것을 "영어의 설계도"라 하겠다. 중학교 1학년부터 토플 문장까지 모든 문장이 영어의 설계도에 포함되어 있다.

우리가 건물을 짓기 전에 무엇이 필요한가? 설계도가 반드시 있어야 한다. 설계도가 있어야 건물을 지을 수 있다. 설계도가 없이 건물을 지을 수 있겠는가? 설계도가 있다는 것은 건물에 끝이 있다는 것을 의미한다. 완성을 의미한다!

영어에 무엇이 있는가? 영어의 설계도가 있다. 영어의 설계도가 있다는 말은 영어에 끝이 있다는 것이다. 영어의 설계도가 있고, 영어의 도면이 있다. 3개월 영어혁명이 가능한 이유는 영어 설계도와 영어 도면이 있기 때문이다.

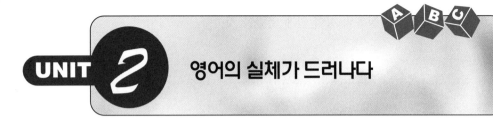

UNIT 2 영어의 실체가 드러나다

영어에는 설계도가 있다. 영어의 설계도가 있다는 말은 영어의 끝이 있다는 것이다.

「ONE STOP ENGLISH」1단계 : 영어 설계도

제1장에서 영어는 "자리언어"라는 사실을 알았다. 영어는 자리언어로 주어자리, 동사자리, 목적어자리, 보어자리, 구자리, 절자리가 있다고 했다. 또 자리언어인 영어는 위치를 잡아줄 수 있는 주어와 동사가 있고 주어와 동사를 중심으로 주어 앞자리, 주어와 동사 사이 자리, 동사 다음 자리가 있다.

영어의 설계도가 있다는 것은 영어에 끝이 있다는 것을 의미한다. 완성을 의미한다! 그렇다면 설계도만 있다고 해서 건물이 완성되겠는가? 설계도를 따라서 땅을 파고 기둥을 세워야 한다.

「ONE STOP ENGLISH」 2단계 : 영어 공식

수학에 공식이 있는 것처럼 영어에도 공식이 있다. 공식이 있다는 것은 답이 있다는 것이다.

> Even in Korea as a matter of fact the education of girls and women was far behind that of boys and men.

이 문장은 중학교 수준의 문장은 아니다. 토익 시험에서 출제된 문장이다. 문장 안에 등장한 단어들은 그렇게 어렵지는 않다.

"in"은 "~의 안에", "Even"은 "~조차, 심지어", "as"는 "~로서", "a matter"는 "사건이나 일", "of"는 "~의", "fact"는 "사실", "the education"은 "교육", "girls and women"은 "소녀들과 여인들", "was"는 "be 동사", "behind"는 "~의 뒤에", 그리고 "boys and men"은 "소년들과 남자들"이다.

중학교 2학년이나 3학년 과정을 정상적으로 공부했다면 알 수 있는 단어들이다. 자, 여기 나와 있는 단어들은 별로 어렵지 않다. 그런데 "이 문장을 해석해 보라."고 하면 해석이 어렵다. "주어를 찾아보라."고 하면 문제는 달라진다.

짧은 문장이든, 쉬운 문장이든, 긴 문장이든, 복잡한 문장이든 그 문장의 주어를 모르면 해석할 수 없다. 그러니까 주어가 중요하다.

주어를 찾아보라고 한 이유는 문장을 해석하려고 할 때 짧은 문장이든, 쉬운 문장이든, 긴 문장이든, 복잡한 문장이든 그 문장의 주어를 모르면 해석할 수 없다. 그러니까 주어가 중요하다. 영작을 할 때도 마찬가지이다.

다음 문장에서 주어를 찾아보라고 하면 세 부류의 학생이 있다.

case 1 "was"의 앞이 모두 주어

case 2 "girls and women"이 주어

case 3 "은, 는, 이"를 붙여서 말이 되면 주어

이 방법으로 단순한 문장에서는 적용이 되지만 길고 복잡한 문장에서는 주어를 찾을 수 없게 된다.

주어를 찾는 공식에는 여섯 가지가 있는데, 여기에서는 한 가지만 이야기 하겠다. 나머지는 본 교재 제3장에서 자세하게 다루어 보도록 하겠다.

> 첫 번째, 주어는 동사 앞에 온다.
> 두 번째, 동사 앞에 있는 명사가 주어이다. 그러나 전치사 +명사의 형태가 되면 이것은 절대로 주어가 될 수 없다.

in Korea(X) as a matter(X) of fact(X) of girls and women(X) the education(0)

따라서 "the education"이 주어가 된다. 이와 같이 문장을 보고 해석할 필요 없이 바로 주어를 찾을 수 있는 방법이 있다.

영어뿐만 아니라 모든 언어는 과학이다. 영어의 체계를 분석한 영어의 설계도 위에 영어의 공식을 가지고 영어의 기둥을 세울 수 있다.

영어뿐만 아니라 모든 언어는 과학이다. 영어의 체계를 분석한 영어의 설계도 위에 영어의 공식을 가지고 영어의 기둥을 세울 수 있다.

주어의 공식 6가지

동사의 공식 8가지

목적어와 보어 공식 18가지

이 공식들을 정복하면 지겨운 영문법이 한 번에 해결된다. 기존의 영어 문법책은 파편식 학습을 요구한다. 예를 들어 일반 문법책은 제1강 동사편, 제2강 명사편, 제3강 대명사편, 제4강 부사편, 제5강 부정사편 등의 순서로 이루어졌다. 그래서 학습자들이 제1강을 공부하고, 제2강을 공부하면 1강이 희미해지고, 제3강을 공부하면 제1강과 제2강이 희미해진다. 그래서 이제까지 공부한 영어책을 보면 앞부분은 공부한 흔적이 있는데 뒤 부분은 전혀 공부한 흔적이 없는 것을 볼 수 있을 것이다.

ONE STOP ENGLISH는 이런 문제점을 완벽하게 해결했다. ONE STOP ENGLISH는 파편식이 아닌 영어 설계도와 영어 공식을 이용하여 통합식 영어학습을 가능케 했다. 그래서 영어가 한 눈에 보이고 영어의 눈과 귀가 열리는 신기한 경험을 할 수 있게 했다.

ONE STOP ENGLISH는 파편식이 아닌 영어 설계도와 영어 공식을 이용하여 통합식 영어학습을 가능케 했다. 그래서 영어가 한 눈에 보이고 영어의 눈과 귀가 열리는 신기한 경험을 할 수 있게 했다.

「ONE STOP ENGLISH」 3단계 : 단어암기법

아무리 영어설계도와 공식을 잘 파악하고 있다고 하더라도 단어를 알지 못하면 아무 의미가 없다. 영어를 공부하는 학생들의 발목을 잡고 있는 것이 단어암기이다. 단어를 모르면 독해가 불가능하고, 단어를 모르면 영문법을 시작할 수 없으며, 영작은 아예 포기할 수밖에 없다. 또한 단어를 모르는데 어떻게 외국인과 대화할 수 있겠으며, 단어를 모르는데 영어방송을 들을 수 있겠는가? 결국 단어 문제 해결이 영어학습의 열쇠라 할 수 있다.

오늘 두 시간을 투자해서 100단어를 외웠다고 하자. 그 단어를 1주일 후에 물어보면 몇 개나 기억하고 있을까? 영어의 기본이며, 영어학습의 기초 체력인 영어단어 암기가 해결되지 않은 채 영어를 시작하니 결국 10년을 공부해도 답이 없이 공회전만 계속하게 된 것이다. 지금까지 우리가 단어를 어떻게 암기해 왔는가?

－학창시절의 단어 암기법－
백지에 쓰면서 암기하는 방법
입으로 중얼중얼 하면서 암기하는 방법
손바닥에 써가지고 다니면서 암기하는 방법
어떤 사람은 단어를 암기하기 위해 사전을 한 장 한 장씩 찢어서 먹었다는 전설적인 이야기도 있다.

독일 심리학자 에빙하우스(Ebbinghous, Herman 1850~1909)의 인간 망각곡선 원리를 활용한 과학적인 단어 암기법

영어단어 암기의 문제가 이제 100% 해결 된다!

지난 5년 동안 평범한 암기력을 가진 학생, 일반성인들을 대상으로 임상실험을 한 결과 거의 99%가 대만족을 했으며, 1주일에 300~500 단어, 3개월에 5,000~6,000 단어를 완벽하게 암기하였다.

다음에 이야기하는 원리를 잘 이해하기 바란다. 독일의 심리학자이며, 베를린 대학교 교수였던 에빙하우스(Ebbinghous, Herman 1850~1909)는 인간의 망각곡선 이론을 발표하였다. 그는 그의 이론에서 인간은 학습 후 20분 이내에 학습 내용의 약 42%, 한 시간 뒤에 56%, 한 달 뒤에 80% 가량을 망각하게 됨을 밝혔다. 망각할 수밖에 없는 인간이 어떤 특정한 것을 지속적으로 기억할 수 있게 하기 위해서는 인간의 망각을 극복할 수 있는 대안이 필요하다. 그것이 주기적인 반복학습의 원리이다.

다음은 단어암기 가상실험이다

A와 B라는 학생을 비교해 보도록 하겠다. 두 학생에게 똑 같은 조건으로 단어를 암기하도록 했다.

목표 : 100개의 단어 암기

기간 : 월~금

암기에 쏟는 시간 : 매일 1시간(60분)

학습성과 확인 : 토요일 TEST

TEST 방법 : sun ➡ 태양

A학생

월	화	수	목	금	토
1~20	21~40	41~60	61~80	81~100	시험

A라는 학생은 월요일부터 금요일까지 100개 단어를 5일 분량으로 나눠서 하루에 1시간을 투자해서 하루에 20개씩 외웠다.

그러나 B라는 학생은 하루에 1~100번까지 암기한 것이 아니고 단지 보았다.

B학생

월	화	수	목	금	토
1~100	1~100	1~100	1~100	1~100	시험

B학생은 보는데 단순하게 보는 것이 아니고 스펠링과 단어의 뜻을 시간 차를 두면서 보았다.

sun ➡ 태양   flowe ➡ 꽃   tree ➡ 나무

이런 식으로 스펠링을 보고 뜻을 보고, 스펠링을 보고 뜻을 보고, 1번부터 100번까지 한 번 보는데 3분 동안 100번까지 보도록 했다. 이 때 주의할 것은 절대로 암기하려고 하면 안 된다. 눈으로 편안하게 보면 된다.

또 한 가지 스펠링하고 뜻을 절대로 동시에 보지 말아야 한다.

반드시 스펠링 ➡ 뜻

시간차를 두고 빠른 속도로 1번 단어부터 100번 단어까지 보아야 한다. 매일 1시간 60분을 암기하는 조건이었으므로 3분에 20회를 반복할 수 있다. 우리가 컵에 물을 따라본 경험이 있을 것이다. 물을 컵에 따르면 물이 점점차서 올라온다. 멈추지 않으면 이 물이 나중에는 넘치게 된다.

똑 같은 원리다. 1번 단어부터 100번 단어까지 "sun ➜ 태양, flower ➜ 꽃, tree ➜ 나무"과 같은 방식으로 여러 번 반복을 하다보면 어느 순간이 되면 "sun"을 보는 순간 "태양"하고 자동적으로 뇌에서 감지가 되는 때가 온다. 이렇게 해서 스펠링을 보는 순간 뜻이 생각나면 이 단어는 외운 단어가 된 것이다. 그렇게 되면 그 단어에 ×표시를 한다.

그 다음에 1번 단어부터 100번 단어까지 반복할 때 × 표시단어는 바로 넘긴다. 그렇게 스펠링을 보면 단어 뜻이 기억나는 단어가 많아질수록 1~100단어까지 3분에 시간이 2분에서 1분으로 단축이 될 것이다. 나중에는 완전이 암기가 될 것이다.

A학생과 B학생 실험결과를 비교해 보자.

A학생
1) 첫째 날에 외웠던 단어들이 시간이 지나면서 망각의 원리에 의해서 점점 사라진다.
2) 둘째 날도 마찬가지 이다.

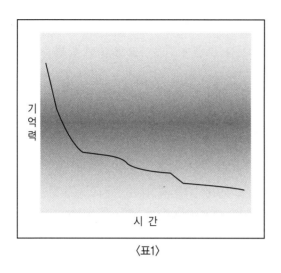

〈표1〉

B학생

1번 단어부터 100번 단어까지 3분에 1회, 하루 20회 반복을 통해서 5일 동안 100회 반복을 한다. 알고 있는 단어는 잠수시키고 모르는 단어만 자동반복을 통해서 영구기억으로 갈 수 있다.

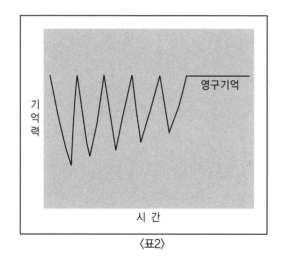

〈표2〉

대학원, 공공기관, 교회 등에서 영어를 배우는 모든 학생에게 이 학습법을 적용한 결과 영어단어 암기를 그렇게 힘들다고 말하던 학생들이 1주일에 300~500단어를 쉽게 암기하게 되었다.

그 중에 특별히 기억에 남는 학생이 있다. 당시 나에게 영어를 배우는 학생들 중에 선화예고 3학년 다니던 정다운이라는 학생이 있었다. 수능시험을 약 2개월 앞두고 영어점수가 오르지 않아 애를 태우고 있었다. 무엇이 문제인지 확인해 보니 독해와 어휘력이었다. 수능시험 2개월을 남겨두고 집중적으로 위와 같은 방법으로 단어암기를 시켜 보았다. 놀라운 것은 하루에 단어 암기에 2시간 투자하고 수능 2개월 앞둔 상황에서 약 4,000단어를 외우게 되었다. 그 노력의 결과는 서울대 음대 합격이라는 열매를 만들어냈다. 물론 다운이의 노력도 있었지만 단어암기 방법이 놀라운 결과를 만들어냈다.

단어 암기에 대한 더 자세한 정보를 얻기 원하는 독자들을 위한 정보
http://www.daum.net에 접속 ➡ 검색창에 「3개월 영어 혁명」을 검색 ➡ 3개월 영어혁명 ➡ 카페 회원으로 가입 ➡ 카페 메뉴 「영어 단어암기 비법」을 클릭

「ONE STOP ENGLISH」 4단계 : 영어문장 해석공식

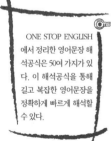

ONE STOP ENGLISH에서 정리한 영어문장 해석공식은 50여 가지가 있다. 이 해석공식을 통해 길고 복잡한 영어문장을 정확하게 빠르게 해석할 수 있다. 수능문장, 토플문장, 영어성경, 비즈니스 영어 등 어떤 영어문장이든 영어문장 해석공식에 적용이 되지 않는 문장은 없다.

이제까지 학생들은 학교나 학원에서 영어를 배울 때 선생님이 해석해 주

는 대로 따라서 해석을 해 왔다. 문제는 수업시간에 배울 때는 해석이 되는 것 같은데 혼자 해석하려고 해보면 쉽게 해석이 되지 않는 경우가 많다. 그러니 영어문장을 해석해 보라고 하면 혼자서 소설을 쓴다.

영어문장을 보면 두려움이 앞서고 자신감을 잃을 때가 많다. 그러나 영어문장 해석공식은 이 모든 문제를 완벽하게 해결해 준다. 영어소설을 읽고 웃을 수 있고, 영어성경을 읽고 묵상하면서 은혜 받을 수 있는 그 꿈같은 일이 현실로 이루어질 수 있다.

「ONE STOP ENGLISH」 5단계 : 영어작문공식

ONE STOP ENGLISH에는 영어작문공식(영작공식)이 있다. 건물을 지을 때 맨 먼저 설계도가 나와야 하고 그 설계도를 가지고 땅을 파고 기둥을 세워야 한다. 기둥을 세운 후 벽돌을 쌓고 지붕을 올린다. 마지막으로 할 일이 내부 장식을 위한 인테리어 작업이다.

이런 과정을 걸쳐서 집을 완성하는 것처럼 영어작문도 이와 같다.

ONE STOP ENGLISH에는 영어 설계도가 있다. 영어설계를 완성시킬 수 있는 영어공식이 있다. 많은 벽돌이 건축에 필요한 것처럼 특허 받은 단어 암기법을 통해 많은 단어를 암기할 수 있다.

집을 건축할 때 인테리어 작업이 있는 것처럼 영어문장 해석공식이 있어 영어문장을 조합시킬 수 있다. 결국 영어 집(영어 영작)이 가능해 진다.

영작이 안 되는 이유는 간단하다. 영어에 대한 밑그림이 없고, 영어 기둥을 못 세우고, 영어단어를 모르고, 영어문장을 조합할 수 있는 능력이 없기 때문이다.

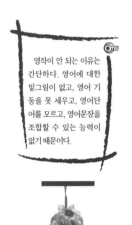

영작이 안 되는 이유는 간단하다. 영어에 대한 밑그림이 없고, 영어 기둥을 못 세우고, 영어단어를 모르고, 영어문장을 조합할 수 있는 능력이 없기 때문이다.

영어의 새로운 지평이 열렸다. 이제 믿음과 확신, 그리고 열정만 있다면 이미 영어는 정복된 것이다.

주어(S)를 찾는 공식

3 UNIT

주어는 문장의 머리와 같다. 문장을 형성함에 있어 가장 중요한 중심부이다. 따라서 주어를 찾는 것은 문장 파악의 열쇠이며 의미 파악의 시작이다. 간단한 문장에서 주어 찾기는 쉽지만 문장이 어려워질수록 주어 찾기는 미로가 되어버린다. 왜냐하면 주어는 종류가 다양하기 때문이다.

> 주어는 문장의 머리와 같다. 문장을 형성함에 있어 가장 중요한 중심부이다. 따라서 주어를 찾는 것은 문장 파악의 열쇠이며 의미 파악의 시작이다.

주어가 될 수 있는 것은 명사와 대명사이다. 그러나 그 명사나 대명사 앞에 전치사가 오면 주어가 아니다.

첫째, 명사 주어

이 세상 만물에는 모두 빠짐없이 이름이 있다! 이처럼 사람이나 사물을 지칭하는 이름을 바로 '명사' 라고 한다.

1) 명사의 종류: 고유, 보통, 집합, 물질, 추상명사

(1) 셀 수 있는 명사 : 단, 복수 가능

✱ many, few로 수식(보통, 집합명사)

✱ 보통명사 : 일반적으로 붙여진 이름. book, dog, boy, mother.

✱ 집합명사 : 하나하나가 모여서 한 집합체를 이룬 것. family, class.

(2) 셀 수 없는 명사 : 단, 복수 없음.

✱ much, little 이 수식(물질, 고유, 추상명사)

✱ 고유명사 : 이 세상에 꼭 하나 밖에 없는 이름이다.

Korea, Japan, Seoul, Kim Chol-Soo, Whitney Houston

✱ 물질명사 : 과학 과목에서 배운 물질이다.

water, milk, sugar, paper

✱ 추상명사 : 눈을 비비고 봐도 보이지 않는다. 다만 머리속에만 있
는 개념이다. 어떻게 셀 수 있겠는가? love, hope,
life

둘째, 대명사 주어

1) 인칭 대명사

말하는 사람인 "나"를 1인칭, 말을 듣는 상대방인 "당신"을 2인칭, 그리
고 그 이외의 "제3자"를 모두 3인칭이라 하는데 이를 구별하여 나타내는
대명사를 인칭대명사라 한다.

(1) 1인칭

주격(~는, ~이, ~가) : I / we

소유격(~의) : my / our

목적격(~을/를, ~에게) : me / us

I lost my way in the woods.(나는 숲 속에서 길을 잃었다.)

We had a good time there.(우리는 그곳에서 즐거운 시간을 보냈다.)

(2) 2인칭

주격(~는, ~이, ~가) : you / you

소유격(~의) : your / your

목적격(~을/를, ~에게) : you / you

You have a nice car.(당신은 좋은 차를 가지고 있다.)

You should help the poor.(여러분들은 가난한 사람들을 도와야 한다.)

(3) 3인칭

주격(~는, ~이, ~가) : he / she / it / they

소유격(~의) : his / her / its / their

목적격(~을/를, ~에게) : him / her / it / them

He is doing his homework now.(그는 지금 그의 숙제를 하고 있다.)

It is very beautiful, isn't it?(그것은 아주 아름답죠, 안 그래요?)

They are afraid of their teacher.(그들은 그들의 선생님을 두려워
한다.)

■ 보충 학습 : 소유격 다음에는 반드시 명사가 와야 한다.

This is not my book.(이것은 나의 책이 아니다.)

Can I use your car?(당신의 차를 써도 되나요?)

His house is near his school. (그의 집은 그의 학교 근처에 있다.)

Her children are still young. (그녀의 아이들은 아직 어리다.)

■ 보충 학습 : 전치사의 뒤에 대명사가 오는 경우에는 목적격을 쓴다.

전치사 뒤에 오는 명사나 대명사는 전치사의 목적이기 때문이다.

I went out for a walk with her. (나는 그녀와 함께 산책하러 나갔다.)

I'd like to talk to him. (나는 그에게 말하고 싶다.)

2) 소유대명사

(1) "인칭대명사의 소유격+명사"를 하나의 독립된 대명사로 나타낸 것을 소유대명사라 하며 "~의 것"이란 뜻을 갖는다.

1인칭 : mine(나의 것) / ours(우리들의 것)

2인칭 : yours(너의 것) / yours(너희들의 것)

3인칭 : his(그의 것) / hers(그녀의 것) / theirs(그들의 것)

■ 보충 학습 : 3인칭 it의 소유대명사는 없다.

My shoes are black, but yours are brown.

(나의 신발은 검정색이지만 너의 것은 갈색이다.)

(2) 소유대명사는 앞에 나온 명사의 반복을 피하기 위하여 사용된다. 따라서 소유대명사는 "소유격+단수명사"의 뜻이 될 수도 있고, "소유격+복수명사"의 뜻이 되기도 한다.

His hat is not <u>mine</u>. (그의 모자는 나의 것이 아니다)

=my hat

My shoes are black, but <u>yours</u> are brown.

=your shoes

(나의 신발은 검정색이지만 너의 것은 갈색이다.)

His house is bigger than <u>hers.</u>(그의 집은 내 집보다 더 크다)

=her house

Our children are cleverer than <u>theirs.</u>

=their children

(우리의 아이들은 그들의 아이들보다 더 영리하다.)

3) 지시대명사 This / That

Learning Point 1 : This와 That

사람이나 사물을 가리키는 대명사를 지시대명사라 한다. this는 시간적, 공간적으로 가까운 것에 대해 쓰고, that은 상대적으로 멀리 있는 것에 대해 사용한다. this의 복수형은 these, that의 복수형은 those이다.

<u>This</u> is bigger than that.(이것은 저것보다 더 크다.)

<u>This</u> is my book, and that is Tom's.(이것은 나의 책이고, 저것은 탐의 것이다.)

4) 부정대명사

부정대명사란 막연한 사람이나 사물-수량을 나타내는 대명사로서. some, any, one, other, another, each, either, neither 등이 있다. 뒤에 명사가 오면 형용사 역할을 한다.

5)의문대명사

누가, 무엇, 어떤 것(사람) 등 의문을 나타내는 명사로서 who, whom, whose, which, what 등이 있다. 그 중에 주어가 될 수 있는 것은 who, which, what이다.

Who went there yesterday?(누가 어제 거기에 갔습니까?)

What has brought you here?(무엇이 당신을 여기로 데려왔습니까?=
여기에 왜 왔습니까?)

Which is taller, he or she?(어떤 사람이 더 큽니까,그입니까 아니면
그 여자입니까?)

전치사 4 UNIT

abc순	단어순	많이 나오는 것	드물게 나오는 것
a	9	at(~에, ~에서), along(~따라서) above(~보다 위에, ~넘어), among=amongst(~사이에) around(~주위에) against(~에 반대하여, ~대비하여) about(~관해서, ~근처에) across(~건너서)	amid=amidst (~사이에)
b	8	beneath(~밑에), below(~보다 아래에) beside(~옆에), between(~사이에) beyond(~넘어서), behind(~뒤에) by(옆에,~까지,~로써)	besides(~외에)

abc순	단어순	많이 나오는 것	드물게 나오는 것
c	1		concerning(~에 관해서)
d	3	down(~아래로), during(~동안)	despite(~에도 불구하고)
e	1		except(~이외에)
f	1	from(~로부터, ~에서)	
i	3	in(~에, ~안에). inside(~안쪽에) into(~안으로)	
l	1		like(~같이, ~같은)
n	2		near(~가까이) notwithstanding(~에 도 불구하고)
o	6	of(~의, ~으로, ~에 관해) over(~위에, ~넘어) on(~에, ~위에), off(~에서, 떨어져서, ~로부터) outside(~바깥쪽에)	opposite (~의 반대편에)
p	1		past(~지나서)
r	2	round(~주위로)	regarding(~에 관해서)
s	1		save=saving (~를 제외하고)
t	4	to=unto(~에. ~으로). toward=towards(~쪽으로) through(~통하여)	throughout (~동안, ~의 도처에)
u	4	under(~아래), up(~위로)	unlike(~에 달리) underneath(~아래로)
w	1	with(~와 함께, ~로써). without(~없이)	
	49	33	16

★ 전치사구

전치사구			
전치사구	뜻	전치사구	뜻
according to	~ 에 의하면	in addition to	~ 에 첨가하여
as for	~ 에 관한	in behalf of	~ 을 위하여
as to	~ 에 관한	in case of	~ 인 경우에
at the back of	~ 의 뒤에	in consequence of	~ 때문에
at the foot of	~ 의 기슭에	in favor of	~ 에 찬성하여
at the top of	~ 의 위에	in front of	~ 의 앞에
because of	~ 때문에	in honor of	~ 을 위하여
by dint of	~ 덕택으로	in pursuit of	~ 을 추구하여
by means of	~ 을 수단으로	in search of	~ 을 찾아서
by way of	~ 을 경유하여	in spite of	~ 에도 불구하고
due to	~ 때문에	instead of	~ 의 대신에
for lack of	~ 이 결핍하여	on account of	~ 때문에
for the benefit of	~ 을 위하여	on behalf of	~ 을 대신하여
for the good of	~ 을 위하여	owing to	~ 때문에
for the purpose of	~ 을 할 목적으로	out of	~ 밖으로
for the sake of	~ 을 위하여	with a view to	~ 을 할 목적으로
for want of	~ 이 결핍하여	with the object of	~ 을 할 목적으로

★ 전치사로 사용되기도 하고 접속사로도 쓰이기도 하는 단어(8개)

before(~전에, 앞에), after(~후에, 뒤에), but(제외하고, 그러나),
for(~위해, ~향해, ~동안, 왜냐하면), as(~로서,~할 때), since (~이래로),
till=until(~까지) than(~보다)(비교급)

★ 위치 전치사 외우기

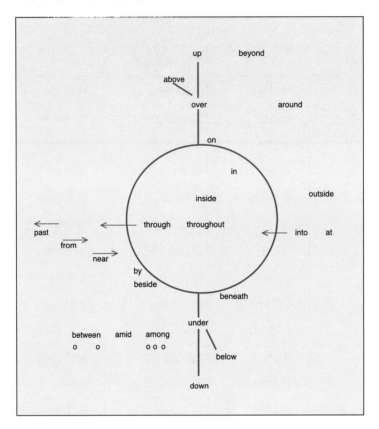

★ 아래 문장에서 밑줄 친 전치사구를 찾아 줄을 긋고 뜻을 적으시오 ★

1. According to my mom, we should be paid more for our work.

2. As for Jane's remarks, I think they were too unfair.

3. Give me a hint as to his identity.

4. He is out because of sickness.

5. There is a lake at the back of the house.

6. They built their base camp at the foot of the mountain.

7. By dint of industry, he has made what he is.

8. Guests have to enter by means of a phone buzzer system.

9. He traveled by way of Italy.

10. Germany was defeated due to lack of goods.

11. They will be released for lack of evidence.

12. Business exists for the benefit of society.

13. In addition to free meals, you are provided with a private room.

14. In case of fire, leave the building immediately.

15. On behalf of the committee, I'd like to thank you for all your hard work.

16. He would park his car in front of my house.

17. The party was held in honor of our teacher.

18. The dog is in pursuit of the cat.

19. The fox scoured about in search of food.

20. He's unable to take part in sports on account of his illness.

21. The accident was owing to careless driving.

★ 명사 주어 예문 ★

1. A car stopped in front of his house.

2. Mary shows me the way to the airport.

3. Jane will take care of our children.

4. The doctor wants to see you.

5. Our children are cleverer than theirs.

6. My shoes are black, but yours are brown.

7. The climate of this country is milder than that of France.

8. Water is composed of oxygen and hydrogen.

9. The milk in the bottle went bad.

10. The beauty of the scenery is beyond description.

11. In the North Atlantic and North Pacific Ocean, all hurricanes are now given girl's name. For years hurricanes in the Caribbean were named after the saint's day on which the hurricane occurred.

12. During the American Revolution the people of Canada remained loyal to England although the rebelling colonies tried to persuade them to join the war for independence.

13. But in 1799 an officer in Napoleon's army discovered near the Egyptian village of Rosetta a smooth, thick black stone covered with carvings that were divided into three separate sections.

3. to부정사 주어

To know oneself is difficult.
  주어   동사 주격보어

= It is difficult to know oneself.
가주어 동사 주격보어   진주어

To take a picture here is forbidden.

To live without water is impossible.

4. 동명사 주어

<u>Walking</u> in the country   <u>is</u>   <u>very pleasant</u>.

     주어   동사   주격보어

= <u>It</u> is very pleasant **walking** in the country.

 가주어   진주어

Reading books is a good hobby.

Being kind to others is good.

5. 절 주어

절이 주어가 될 수 있다. 여기에서 우리가 주목해야 하는 것은 주어절을 이루는 **절단어**가 있다는 것이다. 주어절을 만드는 단어는 **총 18개**가 있다.

* 접속사 : that, whether, if

* 복합관계대명사 : whoever, whosever, whomever, whichever, whatever

* 관계대명사 : what

* 의문대명사 : what, who, whose, whom, which

* 관계부사 : when, where, why, how

[**That he is innocent**] is certain.(**그가 무죄하다는 것은** 확실하다.)

    명사절 (주어)

[**Whoever breaks this law**] will be punished.

    명사절 (주어)

(**이 법을 깨는 사람이 누구든 벌**을 받을 것이다.)

[Whomever you love] will desert you.

    명사절 (주어)

(당신이 사랑하는 사람이 누구든지 당신을 버릴 것이다.)

[Whatever he says] is true.(그가 말하는 것은 무엇이든지 사실이다)

    명사절 (주어)

[Whoever said so] is a liar.

    명사절 (주어)

(그렇게 말한 사람이 누구든지 거짓말쟁이이다.)

6. 비인칭 주어

It is + 날씨, 날짜, 무게, 거리, 명암, 시간 등

It is ten o' clock. (10시이다.)

It is two miles. (2마일이다.)

It is dark. (어둡다)

It is a fine day. (날씨가 좋다.)

비인칭 주어 It은 '그것' 이라고 해석하지 않는다.

아예 없다고 생각하라.

※ 긴 주어를 대신하는 it

부정사, 동명사, 절이 주어로 쓰이면 너무 길어지므로, 주어 자리에 it을 쓰고 원래 주어는 뒤로 보내는 경우가 많다. It으로 시작하는 문장을 대하면 뒤에 부정사, 동명사, 절 등이 나오는지 확인해 본다.

a. It is very easy **to answer** the question, but it isn' t.

b. It is fun **reading** comic books.

c. It is clear from his action **that he loves her**.

★다음의 영어 문장에서 주어를 찾아 선을 그어라.★

1. The spacious room has much furniture.

2. Much clothing is needed in cold countries.

3. To tell him directly will make him angry.

4. She was a mother of three children.

5. To use a bag only once is a waste.

6. Water is composed of oxygen and hydrogen.

7. Asking him the question will be a waste of time.

8. To be always on time is the duty of a gentleman.

9. The water in this glass is not good to drink.

10. The milk in the bottle went bad.

11. The beauty of the scenery is beyond description.

12. To eat too much is bad for the health.

♣단어학습♣

always	부) 늘, 언제나, 항상	angry	형) 노한, 성난
ask	동) ~을 묻다. 부탁하다	bad	형) 나쁜, 불량한 go bad –(음식 등이)상하다
bag	명) 가방	beauty	명) 아름다움, 미
beyond	전) ~의 저쪽에, 너머에, ~보다나은	bottle	명) 병
child	명) 어린이 복수 – children	clothing	명) 의복, 의류
cold	형) 추운, 찬	country	명) 나라, 지방 복수–countries
compose	동) ~을 구성하다, ~의 일부를 이루다 (be composed of~; ~으로 이루어지다)		
description	명) 서술, 기술, 해설	directly	부) 직접적으로, 똑바로, 바로
drink	동) 마시다	duty	명) 의무, 책임, 도의
eat	동) 먹다	furniture	명) 가구
gentleman	명) 신사	glass	명) 유리
good	형) 좋은, 훌륭한	health	명) 건강
him	(he의 목적격) 그를, 그에게	hydrogen	명) 수소(원소 중 제일 가벼운 기체)
make	동) 만들다, 야기하다, 시키다, 되다	mother	명) 어머니, 모친
much	형) (양이) 많은	need	동) ~을 필요로 하다
once	부) 한번, 일찍이, 한때	only	부) 오직, 단지
oxygen	명) 산소	question	명) 질문
room	명) 방, 실(室	scenery	명) 풍경, 경관, 경치
spacious	형) 넓은, 거대한, (도량이)넓은	tell	동) ~을 말하다, 알리다
time	명) 시간, 때, 세월 on time – 정각에	too	부) 매우, 또한, 게다가
use	동) ~를 사용하다, 이용하다	waste	명) 낭비, 동)~을 낭비하다, 허비하다
water	명) 물	wil	(미래시제조동사)~일 것이다

13. [1]In the beginning God created the heavens and the earth. [2]The earth was empty, a formless mass cloaked in darkness. And the Spirit of God was hovering over its surface. (Genesis 1:1~2)

14. [1]So the creation of the heavens and the earth and everything in them was completed. [2]On the seventh day,

having finished his task, God rested from all his work. [3]And God blessed the seventh day and declared it holy, because it was the day when he rested from his work of creation. [4]This is the account of the creation of the heavens and the earth. When the LORD God made the heavens and the earth, [5]there were no plants or grain growing on the earth, for the LORD God had not sent any rain. And no one was there to cultivate the soil. [6]But water came up out of the ground and watered all the land. [7]And the LORD God formed a man's body from the dust of the ground and breathed into it the breath of life. And the man became a living person.[8]Then the LORD God planted a garden in Eden, in the east, and there he placed the man he had created. [9]And the LORD God planted all sorts of trees in the garden—beautiful trees that produced delicious fruit. At the center of the garden he placed the tree of life and the tree of the knowledge of good and evil.[10]A river flowed from the land of Eden, watering the garden and then dividing into four branches. [11]One of these branches is the Pishon, which flows around the entire land of Havilah, where gold is found.(Genesis 2:1~11)

15.[1]In the beginning the Word already existed. He was with God, and he was God. [2]He was in the beginning with God. [3]He created everything there is. Nothing exists that he didn' t make. [4]Life itself was in him, and this life gives light to everyone. [5]The light shines through the darkness, and the darkness can never extinguish it. [6]God sent John the Baptist [7]to tell everyone about the light so that everyone might believe because of his testimony. [8]John himself was not the light; he was only a witness to the light. [9]The one who is the true light, who gives light to everyone, was going to come into the world. (John 1:1~9)

♣단어학습♣

account	명) 설명, 보고	all	형) 전부의, 내내의, 모든
already	부) 이미, 벌써	any	형) 무슨, 조금도
baptist	명) 침례(세례)주는 사람	beautiful	형)아름다운
become	동) ~이 되다, 일어나다		
beginning	명) 시초, 최초 in the beginning-태초에		
believe	동) 믿다	body	명) 몸, 육체
branch	명) 가지, 부문		
breathe	동) 숨쉬다, ~into:~에게 새 생명을 불어넣다		
center	명) 중심, 중앙	cloak	동) (~ in) ~으로 덮다, ~을 은폐하다
come up	동) 떠오르다	complete	형) 완성된, 철저한, 동) ~을 완성하다
create	동) ~을 창조하다, ~을 만들어 내다	cultivate	동) ~을 갈다, 경작하다, 재배하다
darkness	명) 어둠	delicious	형) 맛있는
divide	동) 나누다 ~into ☆ ~을 ☆로 나누다		
dust	명) 먼지	earth	명) (the ~) -땅, 지상, 대지, 육지
east	명) 동쪽	empty	형) 빈, 아무도 없는
entire	형) 전체의, 완전한	everyone	대) 누구든지, 모두
everything	대) 모든 것	evil	명) 악, 악의 형) 나쁜, 악질의
exist	동) 존재하다, 실재하다	extinguish	동) (불을)끄다, 소멸시키다
finish	동) ~을 끝내다, 종결하다	flow	동) 흐르다, 순환하다
form	동) 형성하다	formless	형) 모양이 없는, 실체가 없는
fruit	명) 과일	garden	명) 정원
give	동) ~을 주다	God	명) 신, 하나님, 창조주
gold	명) 금	good	명) 좋은 것, 선 형)좋은, 충분한
grain	명) 곡식알, 낟알	ground	명) 땅
grow	동) 자라다, 발육하다	heaven	명) 하늘, 천국 (보통 the heavens)
hover	동) 공중을 날다, 빙빙 맴돌다 (~over)	itself	대) 그 자신, 바로그것

knowledge	명) 지식, 학문	land	명) 뭍, 육지
life	명) 생명, 삶	mass	명) 덩어리
no	아니오	nothing	대) 아무것도 ~아니다 명)무
place	명) 장소, 동) ~을 놓다, 배치하다	plant	명) 식물 동)~ (씨)를 뿌리다
produce	동) ~을 제조하다, 생산하다	rain	명) 비, 동) 비가 내리다
rest	동) 쉬다, 명) 휴식	river	명) 강,하천
send	동) 보내다	shine	동) 빛나다, 밝게 빛나다
soil	명) 흙, 토양	sort	명) 종류, 품종
spirit	명) 정신, 영혼	surface	명) 표면, 외면, 외관
task	명) 일, 직무	testimony	명) 증언, 증거, 증명
them	대) ((they의 목적격)) 그들을, 그것들을		
there	부) 거기에, (be동사와 함께 존재) 있다		
through	전) ~을 통과하여,~을 통하여	true	형) 참된, 진실의
water	명) 물	witness	명) 목격자, 증인
word	명) 말, 언어	work	명) 일, 노동, 공부 동) 일하다, 작업하다

Amazing Predictions for the Future

Everyone wonders what the future will bring. In your great-grandchildren's lifetime, dinner might be served by robots, and airplanes might fly without pilots. Who knows? Maybe we won't even need airplanes to fly from place to place.

Our vision of the future keeps changing. At your age, your great-grandparents never dreamed that personal computers would receive e-mail letters from anywhere in the world. In the same way, tomorrow's wonders are probably beyond our imagination. Even so, it's fun to try to guess what the future will bring.

COMPUTER-WEAR

In the future, messages from a portable computer may appear on an eyeglass lens. Also, eyeglasses with a camera and speaker in them may whisper into your ear the name of the person you're facing – in case you've forgotten it. Even clothes will be smart. High-tech clothes will warm or cool you any time you want.

VIDEO WRISTWATCHES

In the future, you'll be able to phone home with video wristwatches. At the touch of a button, you'll talk to people across the street or even across the ocean. Smile! A video image of your face will be sent along with your voice.

VIRTUAL REALITY

Suppose you are stuck in the house. Don't be sad. You'll slip on a virtual reality (VR) helmet and enjoy a virtual party with your friends on a computer. You might use a VR helmet to play along inside a television game show, join your favorite rock band onstage, or leap into an action film. The future will be bright for couch potatoes!

DOOR-TO-DOOR DRIVERLESS TAXIS

No cars in the future? No problem! At a taxi station, you'll simply say your destination into a voice-recognition machine. A door will open to a small, automated taxi as the fare is electronically paid from your bank account. Then the taxi will take you to your destination.

MIRACLE CHIPS

"Billy? Where are you?" When a child gets lost, the parents will find him or her without difficulty. Every child will carry a microchip, and it will help the parents to find them. The same kind of chip could also serve as a library card, driver's license, and medical record.

Wonders in the future are probably beyond our imagination. "We study the future so we can prepare for tomorrow," explains Joseph Coates, a futurist from Washington, D.C. Futurists help companies and governments plan ahead — but not too far ahead. Technology is changing quickly, so predictions that look beyond the next 30 years would be mostly guesswork. "Looking into the future is an art, not a science," says Coates.

♣단어학습♣

account	명) 계좌	across	전) ~을 가로질러, 횡단하여
ahead	부) 앞쪽에, 앞으로	airplane	명) 비행기

amazing	형) 놀랄만한	anywhere	부) 어디든지 명) 어딘가
appear	동) 나타나다	art	명) 예술
automate	동) ~을 자동화하다	bring	동) ~을 가져오다, 초래하다
carry	동) ~을 운반하다	chairman	명) 의장, 사회자, 회장
chip	명) 칩, 반도체 소자	company	명) 친구, 동료, 회사
deal	동) 대처하다, 처리하다, 논하다 (~with)		
destination	명) 목적지, 행선지	difficulty	명) 어려움, 곤란
dream	명) 꿈, 동) 꿈을 꾸다	driver	명) 운전자
electronically	형) 전자의, 온라인의	explain	동) 설명하다
eyeglass	명) 외알안경, 접안렌즈	face	동) 마주대하다, 직면하다 명) 얼굴
fare	명) 요금, 운임	fly	동) 날다
forget	동) 잊다 과거-forgot	futurist	명) 미래신자, 인류 진보의 신봉자
government	명) 정부		
grandchild	명) 손자, 손녀 복) grandchildren		
guess	동) 추측하다	guesswork	명) 어림짐작
high-tech	명) 첨단기술	imagination	명) 상상
issue	명) 공포, 발행, 쟁점	library	명) 도서관, 문고
license	명) 자격증	lifetime	명) 일생, 생애
lost	형) 잃어버린, lose의 과거형-잃다	medical	형) 의학의, 의술의
message	명) 알림, 통지, 메시지	miracle	명) 기적, 신기
mostly	부) 대부분의, 주로	next	형) 다음의
ocean	명) 대양, 해양, 바다	pay	동) 지불하다
personal	형) 개인의, 사적인, 개인용의	plan	동) 계획하다
portable	형) 휴대용의, 간편한	prediction	명) 예언, 예보
prepare	동) 준비하다	press	동) ~을 누르다, 밀어 붙이다.
probably	부) 아마도	quickly	부) 빨리
receive	동) 받다	record	명) 기록 동) ~을 기록하다
replace	동) ~을 대신하다, 제자리에 놓다	ruling	명) 지배, 통치 형) 지배하는, 유력한
sad	형) 슬픈	serve	동) ~에 봉사하다,(음식 등을) 제공하다
simply	부) 간단히, 간편하게	slip	동) 미끄러지다
smart	형) 영리한, 빈틈없는	strike	동) ~을 가하다, 공격하다
study	동) 공부하다	suppose	동) ~이라 가정하다, 상상하다
technology	명) 기술	vision	명) 시력, 환상, 통찰력, 미래상
warm	형) 따뜻한	whisper	동) 속삭이다, 밀담하다 명) 속삭임
without	부) 없이	wristwatch	명) 손목시계

Bomba Escapes from the Zoo

When you are writing, ask yourself what your purpose is. Are you writing simply to express your own feelings? Are you writing to give facts and other kinds of information? Are you writing to persuade other people to change their minds about something? The writings that follow are about the same subject. But each has a different purpose. As you read, think about how differently the subject is presented for each purpose.

[1]

I will never forget the first time I saw Bomba the monkey at the Evanstown Zoo. It was a sunny Sunday afternoon. The place was packed with people watching the new monkey. I felt Bomba was doing all of his tricks just for me. If I waved at him, he waved at me. If I scratched my head, he scratched his head. An old man standing by me said, "Well, this monkey sure likes you!"

I never did go to see the zookeepers giving the baby elephant a bath. Instead, I stayed by the monkey cage for two or three hours. I felt sad to leave Bomba, and he seemed sorry to see me go. I promised him I'd be back soon.

Then I got busy with school work, soccer, and all kinds of other things. I was planning to go to see Bomba again this weekend. But now an article in the newspaper says Bomba escaped yesterday. There's a big reward for giving information about

Bomba. I don't want any money. I just want Bomba to be back safely in his cage.

[2]
MONKEY ESCAPES FROM ZOO

A monkey escaped from the Evanstown Zoo yesterday. Zoo officials are offering a $1,000 reward for information.

The spider monkey, known as Bomba, is brown and weighs ten pounds nine ounces. It was born in the zoo and has always lived there.

Andrea Coleman, Director of the Zoo, asks the public not to try to capture the monkey. For the safety of the public and the monkey, special animal handlers will be available 24 hours a day. Anyone having any information about the missing monkey is asked to call Ms. Coleman at the special Missing Animals Hot Line, 555−ZOOS.

[3]

Dear Town Councilman Smith:

The escape of Bomba the monkey from the Evanstown Zoo reminds us that we need more guards at the zoo. Because of outs in funding, the number of zoo guards has been cut in half. Instead of two guards patrolling the zoo grounds, there is now only one. There are two reasons to keep two guards on duty at all times. The first reason is for the safety and protection of the animals in the zoo. The second reason is for the safety and protection of the public. I urge you to vote "yes" on the bill that will provide more funding for the zoo.

♣단어학습♣

영어	뜻	영어	뜻
article	명) 기사, 논설	ask	동) 묻다, 요청하다
available	형) 쓸모 있는, 유용한	bath	명) 목욕
brown	명) 갈색, 밤색	cage	명) 새장, 우리
capture	동) ~을 붙잡다, 체포하다	councilman	명) (지방의회의)의원, 평의원
director	명) 지도자, 지휘자	each	형) 각자의, 각각의
escape	동) 달아나다, 탈출하다	express	동) 표현하다
fact	명) 사실	feeling	명) 촉감, 감각
first	형) 최초의, 첫 번째의	guard	동) 지키다, 보호하다
handler	명) 다루는 사람	information	명) 정보
mind	명) 마음	newspaper	명) 신문
offer	동) ~을 제공하다	official	명) 공무원, 관리
ounce	명) 온스 (무게의 단위)	own	형) 자기소유의
pack	명) 꾸러미, 짐 동) 짐을 꾸리다, 싸다	patrol	동) 순회하다, 순찰하다
persuade	동) 설득하다	promise	명) 약속, 계약 동) 약속하다
protection	명) 보호	provide	동) 제공하다
purpose	명) 목적, 용도, 의도	remind	동) ~을 상기시키다
reward	명) 보수, 보상	subject	명) 주제, 화제
science	명) 과학	scratch	동) 긁다, 할퀴다
second	형) 두 번째의	soccer	명) 축구
special	형) 특별한	spider	명) 거미, 거미 같은 것
stand	동) 서다, 서 있다	trick	명) 책략, 계략, 속임수
urge	동) 재촉하다, 주장하다	vote	명) 투표, ~을 투표로 결정하다
wave	명) 파도, 물결, (손) 흔들기, 동) 손을 흔들다		
weigh	동) 저울에 달다. ~을 평가하다	write	동) ~을 쓰다
yourself	대) 당신자신	zookeeper	명) (동물원)사육사

Growing as a person may take you to new places and present new challenges. These may be stressful, but feeling stress is a natural, necessary part of recognizing a weakness and trying out a new behavior. It is often comfortable and easy to stay the way we are. Giving up old comforts and habits is very hard. It is small wonder that people dislike changing.(수능기출문제)

Since the mid−1990s, teaching Korean to foreigners has made quiet and steady progress. Many universities now offer Korean language programs in Korea and abroad, and many textbooks have been produced for learners of Korean. Only a small number of foreigners, however, have benefited from this progress. Most foreign workers are being taught by Korean co-workers or volunteers who have no or little teaching experience. Thus, it is necessary to establish better educational programs for teaching the Korean language to foreign workers.(수능기출문제)

steady	형) 확고한, 튼튼한	textbook	명) 교과서
university	명) 대학	volunteer	명) 자원봉사자
worker	명) 일(공부)하는 사람		

There was a kind woman who made a last attempt to catch up. Seeing a box of 50 identical greeting cards in a shop, she snapped it up, carried it home, and signed 49 cards before midnight. She posted them the next morning and gave a sigh of relief. Then she opened one remaining card, and found these words printed on it : This little card is just to say a gift from me is on the way.(수능기출문제)

♣단어학습♣

attempt	동) 시도하다, 꾀하다 명)시도	by no means	결코 ~ 않은
catch up	따라잡다	gift	명) 선물
greeting	명) 인사, 절	identical	형) 똑같은, 동일한
last	형) 최후의, 마지막의	post	동) 우송하다
relief	명) 제거, 경감	rush	동) 돌진하다, 갑자기 달려들다 형)바쁜
sigh	명) 한숨 동) 한숨 쉬다, 탄식하다	sign	명) 표, 기호
snap	동) 찰깍하고 소리나다, (~up)을 잡아채다		
well off	부유한		

Thomas Jefferson once said that what matters is the courage of one's convictions. Do you have the courage which comes from the sincere conviction that you are a person of sound character, an honest, dependable, kind, and caring person ? If you do, you will never have to worry about what others think of you. If you know in your heart that you are a good and decent Person, you can life's challenges head-on and without fear of what others think.(수능기출문제)

A terrible accident changed my life. A friend and I were driving home from a midnight movie. As we approached an intersection, we stopped at a red light. No cars seemed to be coming, so I decided to go through the red light. Immediately after we started, I lost consciousness. Later I learned that we had hit a car coming from the other direction. That accident made my friend spend the rest of his life in a wheelchair, and I learned a costly lesson.(수능기출문제)

-고급 문장- 단어학습

1. As the tadpole grows older the cells composing its tail are attacked and absorbed by certain body cells until the tail shrinks and finally disappears completely.[사법고시]

tadpole   올챙이

2. During the American Revolution the people of Canada remained loyal to England although the rebelling colonies tried to persuade them to join the war for independence. [한국전력]

♣단어학습♣

colony	거류민	loyal	충성의
persuade	설득하다	rebel	항거하다
revolution	혁명	surrender	항복하다

3. The Korean economic system does not exist in isolation but is a part of the world-wide economic system. Thus, the economic life of the Korean people is greatly affected by the economic life of all the peoples. [사법고시]

♣단어학습♣

affect	영향을 끼치다	exist	존재하다
isolation	고립	product	농산물
stock market	증권시장		

4. Today, our enormous investment in science and research is the evidence of our faith that science can not only make man richer but it can make man better.[포항공대 대학원]

♣단어학습♣

enormous	막대한	evidence	증거
investment	투자	research	연구

5. But in 1799 an officer in Napoleon's army discovered near the Egyptian village of Rosetta a smooth, thick black stone covered with carvings that were divided into three separate sections.[TOEFL]

♣단어학습♣

carvings	조각	officer	장교
section	부분	separate	분리된

6. In northern countries many insects and worms that cannot live in winter die when cold weather comes. They leave larvae, or egg, to revive their species the following spring. [행정고시]

♣단어학습♣

larvae	유충	revive	소생시키다
species	종, 종류	worm	벌레

7. The animal's mouth is disproportionately large in comparison with his narrow throat. When he fills his mouth with food, he must chew for a long time before he can swallow.[한국외대 대학원, 행정고시]

♣단어학습♣

disproportionately	어울리지 않게	gnaw	갉아먹다
in comparison with	~와 비교해서	swallow	삼키다
throat	목구멍		

8. If democracy is to survive ,above all the thing that a teacher

should endeavor to produce in his pupils is the kind of tolerance that springs from an endeavor to understand those who are different from ourselves.[한양대 대학원]

♣단어학습♣

above all	특히, 우선	democracy	명) 민주주의
endeavor	명) 노력 동)노력하다	spring from	~에서 생기다
survive	동) 살아남다	tolerance	동) 아량, 관용

9. Just when many of the nation's contractors were looking into moving out of the industry, the unfortunate result of the earthquake has created an enormous demand for construction.[TOEIC]

♣단어학습♣

contractor	토건업자, 도급업자	demand	수요
enormous	엄청난	look into	조사하다

10. Drama thrived in India a long time ago, and since the plays presented there always had happy endings, Hindu theatergoers were strangers to tragedies.[외무고시]

♣단어학습♣

costume	명) 의복	theatergoer	명) 관객
thrive	동) 번창하다	tragedy	명) 비극

UNIT 5 동사(V) 찾는 공식

1. be동사(am, is, are, was, were)

2. 일반동사

3. 조동사 + 동사원형

   조동사 : do⟨did⟩, can⟨could⟩, may⟨might⟩, must(have to)⟨had to⟩, will⟨would⟩, shall⟨should⟩, ought to

I can speak French.= I am able to speak French.

She will be able to play tennis.

You may go home now.

You **must keep** your words. = You **have to Keep** your words.

A bear **will not touch** a dead body.

You **shall not kill** any birds here.

You **should be kind** to your neighbors.

We **ought to obey** our parents.

4. 숙어 동사구

동사의 역할을 하는 단어 집단을 말한다.

We **caught sight of** a ship on the sea.

(우리는 바다에 있는 배 한 척을 보았다.)

〈 ☞ catch sight of ~는「~을 보다」라는 뜻의 동사구 〉

They **will take care of** your baby. (그들이 당신 아기를 돌볼 것이다.)

〈 ☞ take care of ~는「~을 돌보다」라는 뜻의 동사구 〉

You **have to ask for** his help. (당신은 그의 도움을 청해야 한다.)

〈 ☞ ask for ~는「~을 요청하다」라는 뜻의 동사구 〉

Would you **turn off** the light? (불을 꺼 주시겠습니까?)

〈 ☞ turn off ~는「~을 끄다」라는 뜻의 동사구 〉

♣단어학습♣

be anxious for	~을 갈망하다	be anxious at (about)	~을 걱정하다
be concerned about (for)	~을 걱정하다	be familiar with	~을 잘 알고 있다
be good at	~을 잘 한다	be possessed of	~을 소유하고 있다
be afraid of	~을 두려워하다	be ashamed of	~을 부끄러워하다
be aware of	~을 알고 있다	be capable of ~을 할 수 있다	
be certain(sure, confident) of	~을 확신하다	be fond o	f~을 좋아하다

be ignorant of	~을 모르다	be proud of	~을 자랑하다
catch up with	~을 뒤따라 잡다	do away with (= get rid of)	~을 그만두다
look down on (= despise)	~을 멸시하다	look forward to	~을 고대하다
look up to	~을 존경하다		
make up for (=compensate for)	~을 보상하다		
put up with (= tolerate)	~을 참다	speak well(ill) of	~을 좋게(나쁘게) 말하다
find fault with	~을 흠잡다	make allowance for	~을 참작하다
make fun of	~을 놀리다	make use of	~을 이용하다
take care of	~을 돌보다	take (a) pride in	~을 자랑하다
be angry with (a person)	~에게 화를 내다		
take advantage of	~을 이용하다, 속이다		
think little of	~을 경시하다	think much of	~을 중요하게 여기다
boast of	~을 자랑하다	call at + (장소)	~를 방문하다
call on + (사람)	~를 방문하다	get on	(차)를 타다
laugh at	~를 비웃다	leave for	~향해 떠나다
listen to	~을 듣다	look after	~을 돌보다
look at	~을 보다	look for	~을 찾다
run after	~을 뒤쫓다	run over(차가)	~을 치다
wait for	~을 기다리다		

★ 다음 문장을 보고 숙어동사구를 찾아 뜻을 쓰시오 ★

1. I am afraid of dogs.

2. He was angry with me.

3. He is anxious at his father's health.

4. They are anxious for freedom.

5. He was ashamed of his failure.

6. He is aware of my presence.

7. She was capable of deceit.

8. He is certain of his innocence.

9. He is familiar with the music.

11. He is fond of playing soccer.

12. He is good at English.

13. She is ignorant of the world.

14. He is possessed of great wealth.

15. You must be proud of your son.

16. She always boasts of her daughters.

17. He called at his office.

18. Dr. Cant called on Jim.

19. You should work harder to catch up with the others.

20. We should do away with the rule.

21. He often finds fault with others.

22. My daughter got on the bus.

23. They laughed at me.

24. Many people leave for America to study.

25. I am listening to the music.

26. I need someone to look after my son.

27. He is looking for a new job.

28. He looked at a picture.

29. You should never look down on others.

30. He is looking forward to meeting you.

31. A boy needs a father he can look up to.

32. You must make allowance for his age.

34. This doesn't make up for his loss.

35. Make use of our information.

36. Mother put up with our arguing.

37. The policeman ran after a criminal.

38. A car ran over the man.

39. Our teacher always speaks well of us.

40. She always takes pride in her work.

41. Take advantage of this chance.

42. She took care of a lot of orphans.

43. He used to think little of his father's advice.

44. I used to think much of my father's advice.

45. I had to wait for him all day long.

5. 12능동, 8수동 시제

12 능동		
기 본	과 거	과거형 (Vd, Ved)
	현 재	현재형
	미 래	will (shall) + V
완 료 have + p.p.	과 거	had + p.p.
	현 재	have (has) + p.p.
	미 래	will (shall) have + p.p.
진 행 be + ing	과 거	was, were + V ing
	현 재	am, are,is + V ing
	미 래	will (shall) be + V ing
완료진행 have been + ing	과 거	had been + V ing
	현 재	have (has) been + V ing
	미 래	will (shall) have been + V ing

12 능동		
기 본 be + p.p.	과 거	was, were + p.p.
	현 재	am, are, is + p.p.
	미 래	will (shall) be + p.p.
완료수동 have been + p.p.	과 거	had been + p.p.
	현 재	have (has) been + p.p.
	미 래	will (shall) have been + p.p.
진행수동 be being +p.p.	과 거	was, were + being + p.p.
	현 재	am, are, is + being + p.p.

6. 조동사 + have + P.P.의 총정리와 문장 전환 공식

1. should (ought to) have p.p.	p.p. 했어야 했는데 (하지 못해 잘못이다) You should have paid your debts. (= ought to)
2. should not have p.p.	p.p. 하지 말았어야 했는데 (해서 잘못이다) You should not have said so.
3. must have p.p.	p.p. 이었음에 틀림없다 She must have been a secret agent. 그녀는 비밀 첩보원이었음에 틀림없다 = She is sure to have been a secret agent.
4. can not have p.p.	p.p. 이었을 리가 없다 He can't have been a thief. 그는 도둑이었을 리가 없다. = It isn't possible that he was a thief.
5. could have p.p.	p.p. 할 수 있었는데 (하지 않았다) We could have bought the car. = We could buy a car, but we didn't.

6. could not have p.p.	p.p. 할 수 없었을 텐데 (했다) We couldn't have persuaded her. =We couldn't persuade her, but we did.
7. may have p.p.	p.p. 했을 것이다. He may have missed the last train. = It is possible that he missed the last train.
8. might have p.p.	p.p. 했을 것이다(약한 추측) He might have missed the last train. = It is possible that he missed the last train. p.p. 했을지도 모른다. (하지 않았다) He might have missed the train.
9. need not have p.p.	p.p. 할 필요가 없었는데 (했다) You need not have bought this car.

7. be 동사 + to부정사가 동사가 되는 경우.

일명 be to 용법이다 : **예정, 의무, 가능, 의도, 운명**

ⓐ He **is to make** a speech next Monday.

He will make a speech next Monday. **(예정)**

ⓑ You **are to obey** your parents.

You must obey your parents. **(의무)**

ⓒ My house **is to be seen** from the station.

My house can be seen from the station. **(가능)**

ⓓ You must work hard if you **are to succeed**.

You must work hard if you intend to succeed. **(의도)**

ⓔ He **was never to see** his country again.

He was doomed never to see his country again. **(운명)**

8. 관용어구 동사 (동사의 원형까지가 동사)

be going to V	~할 것이다
be able to V	~ 할 수 있다
be willing to V	기꺼이 ~하다
be due to V	~할 예정이다
be sure to V	틀림없이 ~하다
be expected to V	~할 것이 기대되다
have to V	~해야만 한다
seem to V	~처럼 보이다
used to V	~하곤 했다
get to V	~하게 되다
need to V	~할 필요가 있다
be supposed to V	~하기로 되어 있다,
be about to V	막 ~하려고 하다
dare to V	감히 ~하다
happen to V	우연히 ~하다
come to V	~이 되다
grow to V	~이 되다
prefer to + V	~을 더 좋아하다
would like to + V	~하고 싶다
had better + V	~하는 편이 낫다
may well +V	~하는 것이 당연하다
may as well + V	~하는 편이 낫다
would rather V@+ than + Vⓑ	~Vⓑ하는 것보다 V@~하는 것이 낫다
can not but + V	~하지 않을 수 없다

1. He is going to meet her.

2. Tim is able to play the piano.

3. He was willing to attend the meeting.

4. He is due to speak tonight.

5. He is sure to come.

6. He is expected to come here.

7. We have to go to New York.

8. He seems to hear someone calling.

9. I used to go to church every Sunday.

10. We need to be successful.

11. You dare to do that.

12 I happened to see him on the street.

13. I grew to realize the delicate situation.

14. You had better take a walk with your son.

15. I would rather die than surrender to the enemy .

16. I prefer to start early.

17. I cannot but admire her good looks.

18. I would like to see the movie with you.

19. We got to be friends.

20. You are supposed to be here at eight every day.

21. I was about to call you.

9. ★ 불규칙 동사(158개) ★

(1) 불규칙 동사 3단 변화

A유형	A → A → A (원형, 과거형, 과거분사형이 같은 것)		

시제	원형		과거형	과거분사형
1	cut	자르다	cut	cut
2	put	놓다	put	put
3	set	놓다	set	set
4	let	기키다	let	let
5	hit	치다	hit	hit
6	shut	닫다	shut	shut
7	hurt	해치다	hurt	hurt

B유형	A → B → B (과거형과 과거분사형이 같은 것)		

시제	원형		과거형	과거 분사형
B-1	d → t → t			
8	build	짓다	built	built
9	send	보내다	sent	sent
10	spend	쓰다	spent	spent
11	lend	빌려주다	lent	lent
B-2	자음~ → 자음ought(aught) → 자음ought(aught)			
12	think	생각하다	thought	thought
13	buy	사다	bought	bought
14	bring	가져오다	brought	brought
15	fight	싸우다	fought	fought
16	teach	가르치다	taught	taught
17	catch	잡다	caught	caught
시제	A		B	B
B-3				
18	keep	지키다	kept	kept
19	feel	느끼다	felt	felt
20	sleep	자다	slept	slept
21	mean	의미하다	meant	meant
22	dream	꿈꾸다	dreamed, dreamt	dreamed, dreamt
23	burn	타다	burned, burnt	burned, burnt
24	learn	배우다	learned, learnt	learned, learnt
25	smell	냄새나다	smelt	smelt
26	meet	만나다	met	met

시제	원형		과거형	과거분사형
27	lead	이끌다	led	led
28	dig	파다	dug	dug
29	strike	치다	struck	struck
30	find	발견하다	found	found
31	say	말하다	said	said
32	pay	갚다	paid	paid
33	lay	놓다	laid	laid
34	sell	팔다	sold	sold
35	tell	말하다	told	told
36	hear	듣다	heard	heard
37	hold	쥐다	held	held
38	lose	잃다	lost	lost
39	stand	서다	stood	stood
40	understand	이해하다	understood	understood
41	win	이기다	won	won
B-8	기 타			
42	shoot	쏘다	shot	shot
43l	leave	떠나다	left	left
44	sit	앉다	sat	sat
45	have	가지다	had	had
46	make	만들다	made	made

C유형	A → B → A (원형과 과거분사형이 같은 것)		

시제	원형		과거형	과거분사형
47	run	달리다	ran	run
48	come	오다	came	come
49	become	되다	became	become

D유형	A → B → C (원형, 과거형, 과거분사형이 다 다른 경우)		

시제	원형		과거형	과거 분사형
D-1	i → a → u			
50	sing	노래하다	sang	sung
51	begin	시작하다	began	begun
52	drink	마시다	drank	drunk
53	swim	헤엄치다	swam	swum
D-2	ow → ew → awn(awn)			
54	know	알다	knew	known
55	grow	자라다	grew	grown
56	blow	불다	blew	blown
57	draw	끌다	drew	drawn
시제	원형		과거	과거분사형
D-3	기 타			
58	be(am, are, is)	이다	was(were)	been
59	break	깨다	broke	broken
60	bite	물다	bit	bitten

시제	원형		과거	과거분사형
61	choose	선택하다	chose	chosen
62	hide	감추다	hid	hidden
63	lie	눕다	lay	lain
64	steal	훔치다	stole	stolen
65	wear	입다	wore	worn
66	bid	명령하다	bade	bidden
67	drive	몰다	drove	driven
68	write	쓰다	wrote	written
69	eat	먹다	atee	aten
70	get	얻다	got	gotten(got)
71	forget	잊다	forgot	forgotten(forgot)
72	go	가다	went	gone
73	fall	떨어지다	fell	fallen
74	ride	타다	rode	ridden
75	rise	오르다	rose	risen
76	see	보다	saw	seen
77	shake	흔들다	shook	shaken
78	take	취하다	took	taken
79	mistake	실수하다	mistook	mistaken
80	do	하다	did	done
81	fly	날다	flew	flown
82	awake	깨우다	awaked	awaked
D-4	～ → ～ed → ～n(ed)			
83	show	보여주다	showed	shown(showed)

E유형	조동사의 불규칙		

시제	원형		과거형	과거분사형
84	can	할 수 있다	could	
85	may	~해도 좋다	might	
86	must	~해야 한다	had to	
87	shall	~할 것이다	should	
88	will	~하겠다	would	

(2) 고급단어편 : 70단어

A유형	A → A → A (원형, 과거형, 과거분사형이 같은 것)		

시제	원형		과거형	과거분사형
1	burst	터지다	burst	burst
2	rid	제거하다	rid	rid
3	shed	흘리다	shed	shed
4	cast	던지다	cast	cast
5	split	가르다	split	split
6	spread	펴다	spread	spread
7	thrust	찌르다	thrust	thrust

B유형	A → B → B (과거형과 과거분사형이 같은 것)		

시제	원형		과거형	과거 분사형
B-1d	→ t → t			
8	bend	굽히다	bent	bent
9	rend	찢다	rent	rent
B-2	자음~ → 자음ought → 자음ought			
10	seek	찾다	sought	sought
B-3	~ → ~t → ~t			
11	deal	다루다	dealt	dealt
12	kneel	무릎 꿇다	knelt	knelt
13	leap	뜀뛰다	leapt	leapt
14	sweep	쓸다	swept	swept
15	creep	기다	crept	crept
16	weep	울다	wept	wept
17	dwell	거주하다	dwelt	dwelt
18	spell	적다	spelt	spelt
19	spill	흘리다	spilt	spilt
20	bless	축복하다	blest	blest
B-4	ee(ea) → e → e			
21	bleed	피나다	bled	bled
22	breed	기르다	bred	bred
23	feed	먹이다	fed	fed
24	flee	도망가다	fled	fled
B-5	ind → ound → ound			
25	bind	묶다	bound	bound

시제	원형		과거형	과거분사형
26	wind	감다	wound	wound
27	grind	갈다	ground	ground
B-6	i → u → u			
28	stick	붙이다	stuck	stuck
29	swing	흔들리다	swung	swung
30	cling	매달리다	clung	clung
31	fling	던지다	flung	flung
32	spin	잣다	spun(span)	spun(span)
33	sting	쏘다	stung	stung
34	wring	비틀다	wrung	wrung
B-7	기 타			
35	awake	잠깨다	awoke	awoke(awoked)
36	clothe	입다	clad(clothed)	clad(clothed)
37	hang	걸다	hung	hung
	hang	교살하다	hanged	hanged
38	behold	보다	beheld	beheld
39	shine	빛나다	shone	shone
	shine	닦다	shined	shined
40	light	밝히다	lit(lighted)	lit(lighted)
41	cleave	쪼개다	cleft	cleft

C유형	A → B → C
	(원형, 과거형, 과거분사형이 다 다른 것)

시제	원형		과거형	과거분사형
C-1	i → a → u			
42	shrink	줄다	shrank	shrunk
43	spring	튀다	sprang	sprung
C-2	ow(aw) → cw → own(awn)			
44	throw	던지다	threw	thrown
45	withdraw	물러나다	withdrew	withdrawn
C-3	~ → ~ed → ~n(ed)			
46	hew	베다	hewed	hewn(hewed)
47	lade	싣다	laded	laden(laded)
48	saw	톱질하다	sawed	sawn(sawed)
49	sew	깁다	sawed	sewn(sawed)
50	sow	씨를 뿌리다	sowed	sown(sowed)
51	mow	베다	mowed	mown(mowed)
52	shave	면도하다	shaved	shaven(shaved)
53	swell	붓다	swelled	swollen(swelled)
C-4	기 타			
54	bear	나르다	bore	borne
	bear	낳다	bore	born
55	freeze	얼다	froze	frozen
56	forbear	견디다	forbore	forborne
57	swear	맹세하다	swore	sworn
58	tear	찢다	tore	torn
59	weave	짜다	wove	woven

시제	원형		과거형	과거분사형
60	forbid	금하다	forbade	forbidden
61	tread	밟다	trod	trodden
62	forgive	용서하다	forgave	forgiven
63	beat	때리다	beat	beaten(beat)
64	overeat	과식하다	overate	overeaten
65	arise	생기다	arose	arisen
66	thrive	번창하다	throve	thriven
67	befall	일어나다	befell	befallen
68	strive	애쓰다	strove	striven
69	undertake	맡다	undertook	undertaken
70	slide	미끄러지다	slid	slidden

★다음의 영어 문장에서 주어, 동사에 찾아 선을 그어라. ★

1. The spacious room has much furniture.

2. Much clothing is needed in cold countries.

3. To tell him directly will make him angry.

4. She was a mother of three children.

5. To use a bag only once is a waste.

6. Water is composed of oxygen and hydrogen.

7. Asking him the question will be a waste of time.

8. To be always on time is the duty of a gentleman.

9. The water in this glass is not good to drink.

10. The milk in the bottle went bad.

11. The beauty of the scenery is beyond description.

12. To eat too much is bad for the health.

♣단어학습♣

always	부) 늘, 언제나, 항상	angry	형) 노한, 성난
ask	동) ~을 묻다. 부탁하다		
bad	형) 나쁜, 불량한 go bad –(음식 등이)상하다		
bag	명) 가방	beauty	명) 아름다움, 미
beyond	전) ~의 저쪽에, 너머에, ~보다나은	bottle	명) 병
child	명) 어린이 복수 – children	clothing	명) 의복, 의류
cold	형) 추운, 찬		
compose	동) ~을 구성하다, ~의 일부를 이루다 (be composed of~; ~으로 이루어지다)		
country	명) 나라, 지방 복수–countries	description	명) 서술, 기술, 해설
directly	부) 직접적으로, 똑바로, 바로	drink	동) 마시다
duty	명) 의무, 책임, 도의	eat	동) 먹다
furniture	명) 가구	gentleman	명) 신사
glass	명) 유리	good	형) 좋은, 훌륭한
health	명) 건강	him	(he의 목적격) 그를, 그에게
hydrogen	명) 수소(원소 중 제일 가벼운 기체)	make	동) 만들다, 야기하다, 시키다, 되다
mother	명) 어머니, 모친	much	형) (양이) 많은
need	동) ~을 필요로 하다	once	부) 한번, 일찍이, 한때
only	부) 오직, 단지	oxygen	명) 산소
question	명) 질문	room	명) 방, 실(室)
scenery	명) 풍경, 경관, 경치	spacious	형) 넓은, 거대한, (도량이)넓은
tell	동) ~을 말하다, 알리다	time	명) 시간, 때, 세월 on time – 정각에
too	부) 매우, 또한, 게다가	use	동) ~를 사용하다, 이용하다
waste	명) 낭비, 동)~을 낭비하다, 허비하다	water	명) 물
will	(미래시제조동사)~일 것이다		

13. [1]In the beginning God created the heavens and the earth.
[2]The earth was empty, a formless mass cloaked in darkness.
And the Spirit of God was hovering over its surface.
(Genesis 1:1~2)

14. [1]So the creation of the heavens and the earth and

everything in them was completed. ²On the seventh day, having finished his task, God rested from all his work. ³And God blessed the seventh day and declared it holy, because it was the day when he rested from his work of creation. ⁴This is the account of the creation of the heavens and the earth. When the LORD God made the heavens and the earth, ⁵there were no plants or grain growing on the earth, for the LORD God had not sent any rain. And no one was there to cultivate the soil. ⁶But water came up out of the ground and watered all the land. ⁷And the LORD God formed a man's body from the dust of the ground and breathed into it the breath of life. And the man became a living person. ⁸Then the LORD God planted a garden in Eden, in the east, and there he placed the man he had created. ⁹And the LORD God planted all sorts of trees in the garden—beautiful trees that produced delicious fruit. At the center of the garden he placed the tree of life and the tree of the knowledge of good and evil. ¹⁰A river flowed from the land of Eden, watering the garden and then dividing into four branches. ¹¹One of these branches is the Pishon, which flows around the entire land of Havilah, where gold is found. (Genesis 2:1~11)

15. ¹In the beginning the Word already existed. He was with God, and he was God. ²He was in the beginning with God. ³He created everything there is. Nothing exists that he

didn't make. ⁴Life itself was in him, and this life gives light to everyone. ⁵The light shines through the darkness, and the darkness can never extinguish it. ⁶God sent John the Baptist ⁷to tell everyone about the light so that everyone might believe because of his testimony. ⁸John himself was not the light; he was only a witness to the light. ⁹The one who is the true light, who gives light to everyone, was going to come into the world. (John 1:1~9)

♠단어학습♠

account	명) 설명, 보고	all	형) 전부의, 내내의, 모든
already	부) 이미, 벌써	any	형) 무슨, 조금도
baptist	명) 침례(세례)주는 사람	beautiful	형)아름다운
become	동) ~이 되다, 일어나다		
beginning	명) 시초, 최초 in the beginning-태초에		
believe	동) 믿다	body	명) 몸, 육체
branch	명) 가지, 부문		
breathe	동) 숨쉬다, ~into;~에게 새 생명을 불어넣다		
center	명) 중심, 중앙		
cloak	동) (~ in) ~으로 덮다, ~을 은폐하다		
come up	동) 떠오르다		
complete	형) 완성된, 철저한, 동) ~을 완성하다		
create	동) ~을 창조하다, ~을 만들어 내다		
cultivate	동) ~을 갈다, 경작하다, 재배하다		
darkness	명) 어둠	delicious	형) 맛있는
divide	동) 나누다 ~into ☆ ~을 ☆로 나누다		
dust	명) 먼지	earth	명) (the ~) -땅, 지상, 대지, 육지
east	명) 동쪽	empty	형) 빈, 아무도 없는
entire	형) 전체의, 완전한	everyone	대) 누구든지, 모두
everything	대) 모든 것	evil	명) 악, 악의 형) 나쁜, 악질의
exist	동) 존재하다, 실재하다	extinguish	동) (불을)끄다, 소멸시키다
finish	동) ~을 끝내다, 종결하다	flow	동) 흐르다, 순환하다
form	동) 형성하다	formless	형) 모양이 없는, 실체가 없는
fruit	명) 과일	garden	명) 정원

give	동) ~을 주다	God	명) 신, 하나님, 창조주
gold	명) 금	good	명) 좋은 것, 선 형)좋은, 충분한
grain	명) 곡식알, 낱알	ground	명) 땅
grow	동) 자라다, 발육하다	heaven	명) 하늘, 천국 (보통 the heavens)
hover	동) 공중을 날다, 빙빙 맴돌다 (~over)	itself	대) 그 자신, 바로그것
knowledge	명) 지식, 학문	land	명) 뭍, 육지
life	명) 생명, 삶	mass	명) 덩어리
no	아니오	nothing	대) 아무것도 ~아니다 명)무
place	명) 장소, 동) ~을 놓다, 배치하다	plant	명) 식물 동)~ (씨)를 뿌리다
produce	동) ~을 제조하다, 생산하다	rain	명) 비, 동) 비가 내리다
rest	동) 쉬다, 명) 휴식	river	명) 강,하천
send	동) 보내다	shine	동) 빛나다, 밝게 빛나다
soil	명) 흙, 토양	sort	명) 종류, 품종
spirit	명) 정신, 영혼	surface	명) 표면, 외면, 외관
task	명) 일, 직무	testimony	명) 증언, 증거, 증명
them	대) ((they의 목적격)) 그들을, 그것들을		
there	부) 거기에, (be동사와 함께 존재) 있다		
through	전) ~을 통과하여,~을 통하여	true	형) 참된, 진실의
water	명) 물	witness	명) 목격자, 증인
word	명) 말, 언어		
work	명) 일, 노동, 공부 동) 일하다, 작업하다		

Amazing Predictions for the Future

Everyone wonders what the future will bring. In your great-grandchildren's lifetime, dinner might be served by robots, and airplanes might fly without pilots. Who knows? Maybe we won't even need airplanes to fly from place to place.

Our vision of the future keeps changing. At your age, your great-grandparents never dreamed that personal computers would receive e-mail letters from anywhere in the world. In the same way, tomorrow's wonders are probably beyond our imagination. Even so, it's fun to try to guess what the future will bring.

COMPUTER-WEAR

In the future, messages from a portable computer may appear on an eyeglass lens. Also, eyeglasses with a camera and speaker in them may whisper into your ear the name of the person you're facing – in case you've forgotten it. Even clothes will be smart. High-tech clothes will warm or cool you any time you want.

VIDEO WRISTWATCHES

In the future, you'll be able to phone home with video wristwatches. At the touch of a button, you'll talk to people across the street or even across the ocean. Smile! A video image of your face will be sent along with your voice.

VIRTUAL REALITY

Suppose you are stuck in the house. Don't be sad. You'll slip on a virtual reality (VR) helmet and enjoy a virtual party with your friends on a computer. You might use a VR helmet to play along inside a television game show, join your favorite rock band onstage, or leap into an action film. The future will be bright for couch potatoes!

DOOR-TO-DOOR DRIVERLESS TAXIS

No cars in the future? No problem! At a taxi station, you'll simply say your destination into a voice-recognition machine. A door will open to a small, automated taxi as the fare is electronically paid from your bank account. Then the taxi will take you to your destination.

MIRACLE CHIPS

"Billy? Where are you?" When a child gets lost, the parents will find him or her without difficulty. Every child will carry a microchip, and it will help the parents to find them. The same kind of chip could also serve as a library card, driver's license, and medical record.

Wonders in the future are probably beyond our imagination. "We study the future so we can prepare for tomorrow," explains Joseph Coates, a futurist from Washington, D.C. Futurists help companies and governments plan ahead – but not too far ahead. Technology is changing quickly, so predictions that look beyond the next 30 years would be mostly guesswork. "Looking into the future is an art, not a science," says Coates.

♣단어학습♣

account	명) 계좌	across	전) ~을 가로질러, 횡단하여
ahead	부) 앞쪽에, 앞으로	airplane	명) 비행기
amazing	형) 놀랄만한	anywhere	부) 어디든지 명) 어딘가
appear	동) 나타나다	art	명) 예술
automate	동) ~을 자동화하다	bring	동) ~을 가져오다, 초래하다
carry	동) ~을 운반하다	chairman	명) 의장, 사회자, 회장
chip	명) 칩, 반도체 소자	company	명) 친구, 동료, 회사
deal	동) 대처하다, 처리하다, 논하다 (~with)	destination	명) 목적지, 행선지
difficulty	명) 어려움, 곤란	dream	명) 꿈, 동) 꿈을 꾸다
driver	명) 운전자	electronically	형) 전자의, 온라인의
explain	동) 설명하다	eyeglass	명) 외알안경, 접안렌즈
face	동) 마주대하다, 직면하다 명) 얼굴	fare	명) 요금, 운임
fly	동) 날다	forget	동) 잊다 과거-forgot
futurist	명) 미래신자, 인류 진보의 신봉자	government	명) 정부
grandchild	명) 손자, 손녀 복) grandchildren	guess	동) 추측하다
guesswork	명) 어림짐작	high-tech	명) 첨단기술
imagination	명) 상상	issue	명) 공포, 발행, 쟁점
library	명) 도서관, 문고	license	명) 자격증
lifetime	명) 일생, 생애	lost	형) 잃어버린, lose의 과거형-잃다
medical	형) 의학의, 의술의	message	명) 알림, 통지, 메시지
miracle	명) 기적, 신기	mostly	부) 대부분의, 주로
next	형) 다음의	ocean	명) 대양, 해양, 바다
pay	동) 지불하다	personal	형) 개인의, 사적인, 개인용의
plan	동) 계획하다	portable	형) 휴대용의, 간편한
prediction	명) 예언, 예보	prepare	동) 준비하다
press	동) ~을 누르다, 밀어 붙이다.	probably	부) 아마도
quickly	부) 빨리	receive	동) 받다
record	명) 기록 동) ~을 기록하다	replace	동) ~을 대신하다, 제자리에 놓다
ruling	명) 지배, 통치 형) 지배하는, 유력한	sad	형) 슬픈
serve	동) ~에 봉사하다,(음식 등을) 제공하다	simply	부) 간단히, 간편하게
slip	동) 미끄러지다	smart	형) 영리한, 빈틈없는
strike	동) ~을 가하다, 공격하다	study	동) 공부하다
suppose	동) ~이라 가정하다, 상상하다	technology	명) 기술
vision	명) 시력, 환상, 통찰력, 미래상	warm	형) 따뜻한
whisper	동) 속삭이다, 밀담하다 명) 속삭임	without	부) 없이
wristwatch	명) 손목시계		

Bomba Escapes from the Zoo

When you are writing, ask yourself what your purpose is. Are you writing simply to express your own feelings? Are you writing to give facts and other kinds of information? Are you writing to persuade other people to change their minds about something? The writings that follow are about the same subject. But each has a different purpose. As you read, think about how differently the subject is presented for each purpose.

[1]

I will never forget the first time I saw Bomba the monkey at the Evanstown Zoo. It was a sunny Sunday afternoon. The place was packed with people watching the new monkey. I felt Bomba was doing all of his tricks just for me. If I waved at him, he waved at me. If I scratched my head, he scratched his head. An old man standing by me said, "Well, this monkey sure likes you!"

I never did go to see the zookeepers giving the baby elephant a bath. Instead, I stayed by the monkey cage for two or three hours. I felt sad to leave Bomba, and he seemed sorry to see me go. I promised him I'd be back soon.

Then I got busy with school work, soccer, and all kinds of other things. I was planning to go to see Bomba again this weekend. But now an article in the newspaper says Bomba escaped yesterday. There's a big reward for giving information about Bomba. I don't want any money. I just want Bomba to be back safely in his cage.

[2]

MONKEY ESCAPES FROM ZOO

A monkey escaped from the Evanstown Zoo yesterday. Zoo officials are offering a $1,000 reward for information.

The spider monkey, known as Bomba, is brown and weighs ten pounds nine ounces. It was born in the zoo and has always lived there.

Andrea Coleman, Director of the Zoo, asks the public not to try to capture the monkey. For the safety of the public and the monkey, special animal handlers will be available 24 hours a day. Anyone having any information about the missing monkey is asked to call Ms. Coleman at the special Missing Animals Hot Line, 555−ZOOS.

[3]

Dear Town Councilman Smith:

The escape of Bomba the monkey from the Evanstown Zoo reminds us that we need more guards at the zoo. Because of outs in funding, the number of zoo guards has been cut in half.

Instead of two guards patrolling the zoo grounds, there is now only one. There are two reasons to keep two guards on duty at all times. The first reason is for the safety and protection of the animals in the zoo. The second reason is for the safety and protection of the public. I urge you to vote "yes" on the bill that will provide more funding for the zoo.

♠단어학습♠

science	명)과학	escape	동)달아나다, 탈출하다
ask	동)묻다, 요청하다	yourself	대)당신자신
purpose	명)목적, 용도, 의도	express	동)표현하다
own	형)자기소유의	feeling	명)촉감, 감각
write	동)~을쓰다	fact	명)사실
information	명)정보	persuade	동)설득하다
mind	명)마음	subject	명)주제, 화제
each	형)각자의, 각각의	first	형)최초의, 첫번째의

pack	명)꾸러미, 짐 동)짐을 꾸리다, 싸다	trick	명)책략, 계략, 속임수
wave	명)파도,물결, (손)흔들기, 동)손을흔들다	scratch	동)긁다, 할퀴다
stand	동)서다, 서있다	zookeeper	명)(동물원)사육사
bath	명)목욕	cage	명)새장, 우리
promise	명)약속, 계약 동)약속하다	soccer	명)축구
article	명)기사, 논설	newspaper	명)신문
reward명)보수, 보상,			

official	명)공무원, 관리	offer	동)~을 제공하다
spider	명)거미, 거미같은것	brown	명)갈색, 밤색
weigh	동)저울에 달다. ~을 평가하다	ounce	명)온스 (무게의 단위)
director	명)지도자, 지휘자	capture	동)~을 붙잡다, 체포하다
special	형)특별한	handler	명)다루는 사람
available	형)쓸모있는, 유용한	councilman	명)(지방의회의)의원, 평의원

remind	동)~을 상기시키다	guard	동)지키다, 보호하다
patro	l동)순회하다, 순찰하다	protection	명)보호
second	형)두번째의	urge	동)재촉하다, 주장하다
vote	명)투표, ~을 투표로 결정하다	provide	동)제공하다

Growing as a person may take you to new places and present new challenges. These may be stressful, but feeling stress is a natural, necessary part of recognizing a weakness and trying out a new behavior. It is often comfortable and easy to stay the way we are. Giving up old comforts and habits is very hard. It is small wonder that people dislike changing. (수능기출문제)

♣단어연구♣

stressful	형)긴장(스트레스)이 많은	natural	형)자연의,천연의,타고난,당연한
necessary	형)필요한, 없어서는 안될	recognize	동)~을보고 곧 알아보다, ~을 인식하다
weakness	명)약함, 허약	behavior	명)행동, 행위, 처신, 행실
often	부)몹시,자주	comfortable	형)쾌적한, 안락한, 편안한
easy	형)쉬운, 용이한	stay	동)머무르다
give up	동)포기하다, 그만두다	old	형)오래된, 늙은
comfor	t동)~을위로하다, 격려하다 명)위로,위안	habit	명)버릇
wonder	명)놀랄만한 것, 경이 동) 이상하게여기다	dislike	동)싫어하다

Since the mid-1990s, teaching Korean to foreigners has made quiet and steady progress. Many universities now offer Korean language programs in Korea and abroad, and many textbooks have been produced for learners of Korean. Only a small number of foreigners, however, have benefited from this progress. Most foreign workers are being taught by Korean co-worker or volunteers who have no or little teaching experience. Thus, it is necessary to establish better educational programs for teaching the Korean language to foreign workers.(수능기출문제)

♣단어학습♣

foreigner	명)외국사람	steady	형)확고한, 튼튼한

progress	명)전진, 진행 동)나아가다, 전진하다	university	명)대학
program	명)프로그램, 계획, 스케줄	abroad	부)해외에, 외국으로
textbook	명)교과서	learner	명)학습자
benefit	명)이익 동)~에게 이익이 되다	worker	명)일(공부)하는 사람
coworker	명)협력자	volunteer	명)자원봉사자
establish	동)~을 수립하다	educational	형)교육상의, 교육적인

There was a kind woman who made a last attempt to catch up. Seeing a box of 50 identical greeting cards in a shop, she snapped it up, carried it home, and signed 49 cards before midnight. She posted them the next morning and gave a sigh of relief. Then she opened one remaining card, and found these words printed on it : This little card is just to say a gift from me is on the way.(수능기출문제)

♣단어학습♣

by no means	결코 ~ 않은	well off	부유한
rush	동)돌진하다, 갑자기 달려들다 형)바쁜	last	형)최후의, 마지막의
attempt	동)시도하다, 꾀하다 명)시도	catch up	따라잡다
identical	형)똑같은, 동일한	greeting	명)인사, 절
snap	동)찰칵하고 소리나다 (~up)을잡아채다	sign	명)표, 기호
post	동)우송하다	sigh	명)한숨 동)한숨쉬다,탄식하다
relief	명)제거, 경감	gift	명)선물

Thomas Jefferson once said that what matters is the courage of one's convictions. Do you have the courage which comes from the sincereconviction that you are a person of sound character, an honest, dependable,kind, and caring person ? If you do, you will never have to worry about what others think of you. If you know in your heart that you are a good and decent Person, you can life's challenges head-on and without fear of what others think.(수능기출문제)

A terrible accident changed my life. A friend and I were driving home from a midnight movie. As we approached an intersection, we stopped at a red light. No cars seemed to be coming, so I decided to go through the red light. Immediately after we started, I lost consciousness. Later I learned that we had hit a car coming from the other direction. That accident made my friend spend the rest of his life in a wheelchair, and I learned a costly lesson.(수능기출문제)

-고급 문장-

1. As the tadpole grows older the cells composing its tail are attacked and absorbed by certain body cells until the tail shrinks and finally disappears completely. [사법고시]

♣단어학습♣
· tadpole : 올챙이   · cell : 세포
· absorb : 흡수하다   · shrink : 줄어들다   · resume : 되찾다.

2. During the American Revolution the people of Canada remained loyal to England although the rebelling colonies tried to persuade them to join the war for independence.
[한국전력]

♣단어학습♣
· revolution : 혁명   · loyal : 충성의
· rebel ; 항거하다   · colony : 거류민
· persuade : 설득하다   · surrender : 항복하다

3. The Korean economic system does not exist in isolation but is a part of the world-wide economic system. Thus, the economic life of the Korean people is greatly affected by the economic life of all the peoples. [사법고시]

♣단어학습♣
· exist : 존재하다   · isolation : 고립
· affect : 영향을 끼치다   · product : 농산물
· stock market : 증권시장

4. Today, our enormous investment in science and research is the evidence of our faith that science can not only make man richer but it can make man better. [포항공대 대학원]

♣단어학습♣
· enormous : 막대한 · investment : 투자
· research : 연구 · evidence : 증거

5. But in 1799 an officer in Napoleon's army discovered near the Egyptian village of Rosetta a smooth, thick black stone covered with carvings that were divided into three separate sections. [TOEFL]

♣단어학습♣
· officer : 장교 · carvings : 조각
· separate : 분리된 · section : 부분

6. In northern countries many insects and worms that cannot live in winter die when cold weather comes. They leave larvae, or egg, to revive their species the following spring. [행정고시]

♣단어학습♣
· worm : 벌레 · larvae : 유충
· revive : 소생시키다 · species : 종, 종류

7. The animal's mouth is disproportionately large in comparison with his narrow throat. When he fills his mouth with food, he must chew for a long time before he can swallow. [한국외대 대학원, 행정고시]

♣단어학습♣
· disproportionately : 어울리지 않게
· in comparison with : ～와 비교해서

· throat ; 목구멍 · gnaw : 갉아먹다
· swallow : 삼키다

8. If democracy is to survive ,above all the thing that a teacher should endeavor to produce in his pupils is the kind of tolerance that springs from an endeavor to understand those who are different from ourselves. [한양대 대학원]

♣단어학습♣
· democracy : 민주주의   · survive ; 살아남다
· above all : 특히, 우선   · endeavor : 노력, 노력하다
· tolerance : 아량, 관용   · spring from : ～에서 생기다

9. Just when many of the nation's contractors were looking into moving out of the industry, the unfortunate result of the earthquake has created an enormous demand for construction. [TOEIC]

♣단어학습♣
· enormous : 엄청난   · contractor : 토건업자, 도급업자
· look into : 조사하다   · demand : 수요

10. Drama thrived in India a long time ago, and since the plays presented there always had happy endings, Hindu theatergoers were strangers to tragedies. [외무고시]

♣단어학습♣
· thrive : 번창하다   · theatergoer : 관객
· tragedy : 비극   · costume : 의복

UNIT 6 형용사, 부사

형용사란?

　형용사란 **명사를 자세히 말해** 주는 역할을 하며 이것을 가리켜 명사를 꾸민다(수식한다)라고 표현 한다. "산이 있다"라는 말과 "푸른 산이 있다"는 말을 비교해 보면 "푸른"이 "산"을 자세히 표현해 주고 있다.

1. 형용사의 세 가지 종류

　1) 성질이나 상태를 나타내는 형용사

large, kind, cold, blue, interesting, tired, sleeping, American, British.

2) 수량을 나타내는 형용사

(1) 수사에는 기수와 서수가 있다.

기수 : one, two, three, four, five…

서수 : first, second, third, fourth, fifth…

(2) 정해지지 않은 수량을 나타내는 형용사

some(긍정문), any(부정문, 의문문)

few(셀 수 있는 것) – a few(긍정), few(부정)

little(셀 수 없는 것) – a little(긍정), little(부정)

many(셀 수 있는 것), much(셀 수 없는 것)

3) 지시형용사 (대명사이지만 형용사 역할을 하는 것)

this(these), that(those), all, each.

* This book is yours. (형용사) This is your book. (대명사)

2. 형용사의 세 가지 위치

1) 명사 앞 (명사를 꾸민다)

An **honest** + boy (정직한 소년)

My **good** + friend. (내 좋은 친구)

2) 명사 뒤 : 후치 수식 형용사(구)

(1) 명사의 접미어가 ?where, –body, –one, –thing으로 끝나는 명사

(everywhere, everybody, everyone, everything/ somewhere, somebody, someone, something/ anywhere, anybody, anyone, anything/ nowhere, nobody, no one, nothing)를 수식하는 일반 형용사는 이러한 명사 뒤에 위치하여 명사를 후치 수식하며, 이러한 명사들의 수는 **항상 단수 취급**한다.

Anyone **intelligent** can do it.
(지적인 사람은 누구나 그것을 할 수 있다.)
I will tell you *something* **very important**.
(나는 너에게 매우 중요한 것을 말할 것이다.)
There is *nothing* **wrong** with the machine.
(그 기계는 아무 이상이 없다.)
Is there *anything* **interesting** in the newspaper?
(신문에 재미있는 것이 났나?)

(2) 형용사 뒤에 형용사를 수식하는 구(전치사+명사)가 뒤따를 때
  Alfred was a king *anxious* for his people's welfare
  (알프레드는 백성들의 복지를 걱정하는 왕이었다.)
  He is a man *greedy* for money.
  (그는 돈에 대해 탐욕스러운 사람이다)
  She has a basket *full* of fruit.
  (그녀는 과일로 가득 찬 바구니를 가지고 있다)
  This is a book *useful* for children.
  (이것은 아이들에게 유용한 책이다)

(3) 측정표시 단위가 올 때

A river two hundred miles *long*　　(200마일 길이의 강)

A road fifty feet *wide*　　(50피트 넓이의 도로)

A man eighty-five years *old*　　(85세의 사람)

A building ten stories *high*　　(10층 높이의 건물)

A bird four feet *tall*　　(4피트 키의 새)

A book one foot *thick*　　(1피트 두께의 책)

A hole three feet *deep*　　(3피트 깊이의 구멍)

(4) 두 개 이상의 유사한 의미의 형용사가 연속될 때

He is a writer *witty* and **wise**.

(그는 재미있고 현명한 작가이다)

He is a face *thin* and **worn**.

(그는 마르고 야윈 얼굴이다)

3) 동사 뒤 : 주어가 어떠어떠하다고 설명하는 서술 용법

[주어 + **be동사** + 형용사]

　　(동사 뒤에 보어만 오는 5가지 경우 참조-82p)

He is happy.

The story is interesting.

3. 형용사 순서

(1) 관사 or 지시형용사 + 수량형용사 + 성질·상태 형용사

these two big cars

(2) 관사 or 소유격 + 부사 + 형용사 + 명사

my very beautiful car.

부사란 무엇인가?

부사는 문장에서 '언제', '어디서', '어떻게', '얼마나' 등을 나타낸다.

1. 다양한 부사들

부사종류	의미
1) 시간부사	now(지금), then(그때에), ago(-전에), yesterday(어제), today(오늘), tomorrow(내일), soon(곧), last(마지막)
2) 장소부사	there(거기에), here(여기에), home(집에), in(안에), out(밖에), far(멀리), forward(앞쪽에), backward(뒤쪽에)
3) 정도부사	very(매우), much(많이), also(역시), too(또한), still(여전히), enough(충분히), almost(거의), even(조차도)
4) 방법부사	fast(빨리), quickly(빠르게), slowly(천천히), well(잘), hard(열심히, 어렵게), carefully(조심스럽게)
5) 결과부사	thus(이리하여), therefore(그러므로).
6) 부정부사	never, little(거의~하지 않는다) seldom, hardly, scarcely, rarely, so not(좀처럼~않다)

부사종류	의미
7) 빈도부사	always, often(자주), usually(대개), once(한번), sometimes(때때로), ever(이제까지)
8) 문두부사	perhaps(아마도), naturally(당연히)
9) 형용사 + ly	large(큰) + ly largely(크게), happy(행복한)+ly->happily(행복하게)

2. 비슷해서 틀리기 쉬운 부사들

1) very와 much 둘 다 "매우"라는 뜻이 있다.

◆very는 형용사, 부사 앞에 온다.

He is _very_ tall, he went _very_ safely.

◆much는 비교급 (~er) 앞에 온다.

He is _much_ taller than I.

2) too와 either 둘 다 '또한'이라는 뜻이 있다.

◆too는 긍정문에 쓰인다.

I can swim, _too_.

◆either는 부정문에 쓰인다.

I can't swim, _either_.

3) enough(충분히)는 **언제나 형용사, 부사 뒤**에 온다.

This room is **warm** _enough_. (형용사 + enough)

He studied **hard** *enough*. (부사 + enough)

** 주의 **

enough가 형용사로 '충분한' 으로 쓰일 때 명사 앞과 뒤에 모두 올 수 있다.

He has *enough* money to buy a home.

(그는 집을 살만한 충분한 돈을 가지고 있다.)

4) already와 yet은 둘 다 '이미, 벌써, 아직' 이라는 뜻이 있다.

◆already는 긍정문에 쓰인다.

◆yet은 부정문, 의문문에서 쓰인다.

The bell has *already* rung.

(종이 이미 울렸다.)

The bell has not rung *yet*.

(종이 아직 울리지 않았다.)

Has the bell rung *yet*?

(종이 벌써 울렸니?)

5) Just와 Just now 둘 다 '막', '방금' 의 뜻이 있다.

◆현재, 현재완료에 Just가 쓰이고, 과거에는 Just now가 쓰인다.

I have *just* arrived here.→나는 방금 여기에 도착했었다.

(현재완료)

I arrived here *just now*.→나는 방금 여기에 도착했다.(과거)

목적어(O)와 보어(C)를 찾는 공식

7 UNIT

목적어 (O)와 보어(C)를 찾는 방법

　O와 C를 찾는 것은 S와 V를 찾는 것만큼 중요하다. 우리는 앞 단원에서 S와 V를 영어문장에서 찾는 연습을 하였다. 이제, 문장의 주요소인 O와 C를 찾는 연습을 통해서 영어문장의 핵심 요소인 S, V, O, C를 자신감을 가지고 모든 영어문장에서 찾을 수 있다. 반복 학습을 통해 이 과정을 철저하게 익히면 영어성경, 영어잡지, 영어소설, 영어신문이 서서히 보이기 시작할 것이다.

1. 문장에서 목적어만 나오는 경우 7가지

1) 일반동사 + **명사 · 대명사**

O

She introduced **her brothers and sisters** to me.

This bus takes **you** to the station.

2) 숙어동사 (을 ~ 다) + **명사 · 대명사**

O

She got over **the handicap** of being blind.

My father took care of **my cousins**.

3) 부정사만 목적어로 취하는 동사 : want, wish, attempt, ask, long, plan,
desire, expect, hope, promise, manage, agree, refuse, fail, care, decide,
demand, determine, choose, learn + to 부정사 목적어

〈예문〉

It promises **to be** warm this afternoon.

She wants **to go** to Italy.

We hope **to see** you soon.

She wishes **to be** alone.

I expect **to be** back on Sunday.

What do you intend **to do** today?

We agreed **to start** early.

He determined **to learn** Greek.

He learned **to drive** a car.

I refused **to discuss** the question.

I don't choose **to be** a candidate.

The boy decided **to become** a sailor.

He never fails to write **to his** mother every week.

We're planning **to visit** Africa this summer.

We desire **to be** happy.

She longed **to say** something.

He asked **to see** the paper.

He attempted **to solve** a problem.

The policeman demanded **to know** where he lived.

Don't forget **to post** the letter.

Nobody cares **to drive** alone such a rainy night.

쉬운 암기법 (to 부정사를 목적어로 받는 동사)

일년 내내 오랫동안(long) 간절히(desire) 세뱃돈 받기만 원하고(want) 바라고 (wish) 소원하고(hope) 기대했는데(expect) 왜냐구요? 친구랑 해외여행 계획하기로 (plan) 약속했거든요(promise). 어떤 친구는 그 여행에 동의하지 않고(agree) 거절 해버렸어요(refuse). 뭐 어른들이 돌보지 않으면(care) 그 여행 실패(fail)하기 십상 이라나요. 그러나 해외여행도 운영하기(manage) 나름, 우선 코스를 잘 선택해서 (choose) 그곳의 문화와 역사를 잘 배워두기로(learn) 결심결정하세요(determine, decide). 그리고 비자가 요구될 테니(demand) 구청에 가서 서류를 요청해서(ask) 당장 해외여행을 시도(attempt)하세요.

4) 동명사만을 목적어로 취하는 동사 : enjoy, mind, avoid, miss, postpone, put off, deny, finish, consider, suggest, appreciate, celebrate, keep on, favor, include, involve, anticipate, stop + **동명사 목적어**

He has finished **working** his duty.

They enjoyed **driving** on the new highway.

I don't mind **smoking** here.

He must not postpone **answering** her letter any longer.

She denied **having** stolen anything.

You must avoid **swimming** in the sea.

He never misses **going** to church every Sunday.

He is considering **going** with his mother.

Why have they delayed **opening** the new school?.

I enjoyed **having** a long chat with Emily.

쉬운 암기법 (동명사를 목적어로 받는 동사)

> 　친구의 호의는(favor) 부인하거나(deny) 피하지 마세요(avoid). 그냥 감사하면서 (appreciate) 즐기세요(enjoy). 생일을 축하한다고(celebrate) 마음(mind)을 다해 제안한(suggest) 파티를 한번 고려해보겠노라(consider). 계속(keep on) 미루거나 (postpone) 연기하면 (put off) 친구사이 이제 끝내고 그만두자(stop, finish)는 거지요. 사소한 감정에 연루되어(involve) 자꾸 miss를 남발하면 천하의 졸장부에 포함(include)되는 거랍니다.

★ 동명사 관용어구

be used to + ~ing(~하는 데 익숙하다)

He is **used to walking** to and from school

looking forward to (~하기를 고대하다)

He is looking forward to seeing you again

feel like + ~ing(~하고 싶다)

I **felt like laughing** at the funny sight.

on/upon+~ ing(~하자 마자)

On finding the news true, he began to run away.

It is no use/good + ~ ing(~해봤자 소용없다)

It is no use/good crying over spilt milk.

waste/spend + O(명사) + ~ ing(~하는 데 낭비하다)

Don't **waste time (on) doing** trifles.

She **spends too much time in dressing** herself.

remember <u>to V</u>

I **remember to see** her tomorrow(미래).

remember <u>V ing</u>

I **remember seeing** her yesterday(과거).

forget <u>to V</u>

I <u>forgot to post</u> the letter(tomorrow).

forget <u>V ing</u>

I <u>forgot posting</u> the letter(yesterday).

stop <u>to V</u>

I <u>stopped to smoke</u>.(나는 담배를 피우기 위하여 멈추었다.)

stop <u>V ing</u>

I <u>stopped smoking</u>.(나는 담배를 피우는 것을 멈추었다.)

like <u>to V</u>

I don't <u>like smoking</u>.   (나는 흡연을 싫어한다)

like <u>V ing</u>

I don't <u>like to smoke</u> now. (나는 지금 담배를 피우고 싶지 않다 : 행동자체)

5) 부정사나 동명사를 모두 목적어로 취하는 동사: begin, start, continue, help, cease, try, hate, like, prefer, propose, love + to부정사, 동명사 목적어

쉬운 암기법 (to 부정사와 동명사를 목적어로 받는 동사) 좋아서

> 좋아서(like) 사랑하게(love) 되면 프로포즈(propose) 시도(try)를 시작(begin, start)하지요. 사귀다가 미워지면(hate) 관계를 그만두지만(cease) 그러나 더 좋아지면(prefer) 결혼해서 계속(continue) 사는 거지요.

<u>The women began to laugh.(laughing)</u>

<u>I continued to read(reading) at home all day</u>.

6) 일반동사 + 절(절단어+S+V+★)

       절 목적어

I believe [that he is innocent of the crime.]

He only did [what he should do.]

I wondered [where he had bought his nice tie.]

He did not know [how he played.]

7) 수여동사 give, tell, send, bring, teach, ask, allow, grant, lend, offer, pay,

   serve, promise, show··· + 명사 + 명사 * 명사절(that,if··· + S + V)

               ~에게   ~을,를

쉬운 암기법(수여동사)

> 사랑은 주고(give) 주기를(grant) 허락하는 것(allow), 말없는 약속(promise)으로
> 서로를 섬기고(serve) 구하여(ask) 얻기보다(get) 빌려주고(lend) 보내주는(send)
> 것, 하늘로서 가져와(bring) 가르치며(teach) 말(tell)로만 아니라 몸소 대가를 지불
> 하여(pay) 보여주신(show) 십자가 사랑의 제안(offer)

She brought her daughter a new dress.

Our teacher taught us the meaning of life.

His mother told him a story.

<u>He</u> asked **me a question**.

2. 문장에서 목적어와 보어가 같이 나오는 경우 5가지

1) S + V + <u>명사</u> + <u>명사</u>

         O   C

첫 번째 명사에는 '-을' 붙이고 그 다음 명사에 '-으로'를 붙여 말이 되면 첫 번째는 목적어이고 두 번째는 보어가 된다. (목적어와 목적보어는 동격 관계이다.)

<u>His father</u> **made** <u>him</u> a doctor.

<u>We all</u> **considered** <u>him</u> a good-natured fellow.

2) S + V + <u>명사</u> + <u>형용사</u>

목적보어가 형용사인 경우 목적어의 상태, 성질을 나타낸다

<u>I</u> will **make** <u>her</u> <u>happy</u>.

3) S + V + <u>명사</u> + <u>to 부정사</u>

         O   C

목적어를 주어처럼 해석하고, to 부정사가 목적어처럼 해석이 된다

* to부정사를 보어로 취하는 동사 *

◆해당동사: advise, allow, ask, beg, beseech, cause, challenge,

command, compel. direct, drive, enable, entice, entitle, encourage, entreat, expect, forbid, force, impel, implore, incite, induce, instruct, intend, invite, lead, oblige, order, permit, persuade, press, request, tell, tempt, urge, warn, want.

** 쉬운 암기법 **(to 부정사를 목적보어로 받는 동사)

1. 우리 코를 자극(incite)하는 음식냄새는 언제나 먹을 것을 기대하도록(expect) 이끈다(lead).
2. 배고픈 사람은 음식을 애(beg)걸(beseech)복(entreat)걸(implore) 요청(request) 한다지만 싫은 음식 억지로(compel) 강제로(impel) 마구(urge) 떠밀어(oblige) 넣듯 먹지 마세요. 그것 때문에(cause) 병나요.
3. 자꾸 먹고 싶은 욕구는 힘으로만(force) 누르지(press) 말고 적당히 허용(permit) 허락(allow)하세요.
4. 다이어트 하는 친구에겐 먹고 싶은 도전적인(challenge) 유혹(tempt)과 꾀임(entice)에 넘어가지 말라고 설득하고(persuade) 타이르세요(induce) 그러면서 "넌 할 수 있다"(enable) 용기를 북돋우세요(encourage).
5. 전국 음식점 정보를 구한다면(ask) 인터넷이 맛집 드라이브(drive) 코스를 친절히 가르쳐주고(instruct) 길도 지시해(direct) 주지요.
6. 식당에 초대받아(invite) 가서는 음식을 주문할(order) 때 명령(command)하듯 하면 안 된다고 충고(advise)해 주세요.
7. 외국여행을 원하는(want) 사람에게는 그곳에서 금하는(forbid) 음식을 먹으면 경고(warn)받는다고 말해(tell)주세요. 그런 사람 여행 자격(entitle) 없지요.

She **wants** me **to go** with her.

She **expects** her husband **to return**.

I **asked** him **to do** that.

Allow me **to introduce** to you my friend, Tom.

I couldn't **force** myself **to sleep**.

The doctor **ordered** the patient **to take** a long rest.

Tell him **to wait**.

Good health **enabled** him **to carry out** the plan.

I **forbid** you **to use** that word.

We **advised** them **to start** early.

I **want** you **to come** here tomorrow.

He **ordered** me **to do** this work.

Doctor **told** me **to keep** my teeth clean.

4) S + V + 명사 + 원형부정사

                O   C

목적어를 주어처럼 해석, 원형 부정사가 목적어처럼 해석이 된다.

*원형 부정사를 보어로 취하는 동사 *

◆지각동사 : perceive, feel, hear, listen to, see, watch, look at,
　　　　　　notice behold, observe

◆사역동사 : let, make, have, help, bid(준사역동사)

** 쉬운 암기법 **

> 아는 것(notice)은 하나요, 느낌(feel, perceive)은 둘이요, 듣는 것(hear, listen
> to)도 둘인데 보는 것(see, watch, look at, behold, observe)은 다섯이라. 가진 것
> (have)으로 도와서(help) 만들라고(make) 시켰으면(let) 명령에(bid) 따르라.

He didn't **see** me **leave** there all alone.

You **heard** him **go out**.

I **watched** him **cross** the street.

He **felt** his heart **beat** wildly.

I have never **observed** him **do**.

I **noticed** the boy **take** the apple.

Her father **lets** her **go** to the dance party.

What has **made** you **come** here?.

Have him **come** here at five.

He **bade** me **come** in.

I **helped** him **find** his things

→ I **helped** him to **find** his things.

※ get의 특별용법 ※

I got him to clean my shoes.-능동

We got his wrist broken-수동

We **felt** the ship **move**.

She **let** us **use** the kitchen.

cf. bid, help 는 원형 부정사, to 부정사 둘 다 취할 수 있다.

** 주의 ** 사역동사 Have의 특별 용법

① have + O(사람) + 원형부정사

② have + O(사물) + 과거분사 : (O가 되게 하다. O가 -되어지다.)

She had **her daughter** wash the dishes.

He had **the car washed** by Tom.

(그는 차가 Tom에 의해 세차되게 했다. 즉 Tom이 세차하도록 시켰다.)

I had **my brother fix** the radio (나는 형이 라디오를 고치도록 시켰다.)

I had **the radio fixed** by my brother.

He had **his hair cut** yesterday. (그는 어제 이발했다.)

She had **her bag stolen** in the bus. (그녀는 버스에서 도둑맞았다.)

5) S + V + 명사 + 분사

             O   C

목적어를 주어처럼 해석, 분사를 목적어처럼 해석한다.

※ 현재분사, 과거분사가 보어로 등장하는 경우는 대부분 지각동사, 사역동사이다.

I **caught** him **cheating** in the exam.

= he **was cheating**.

I **saw** her **beating** a boy.

= she was beating a boy.

I **saw** her **beaten** by a man.

= she was beaten by a man.

3. 문장에서 보어만 나오는 경우 6가지

1) be, become + 명사 · 대명사

            C

He became a teacher.

This car is mine.

2) V + 형용사

        C

* 형용사를 보어로 취하는 동사 *

prove, come, come out, turn out, continue, keep, remain, appear, look, seem, be, become, get, go, make, grow, turn, fall, stay, run, marry, smell, sound, feel, taste, stand, sit, lie, live, die

The plan **proved** **useless**.

He **felt** **hungry**.

She **looks** **healthy**.

3) V + 분사

        C

* 분사를 보어로 취하는 동사 *

prove, come, come out, turn out, , keep, remain, appear, look, seem, get, go, make, grow, turn, fall, stay, run, marry, smell, sound, feel, taste, stand, sit, lie, live, die.

** 쉬운 암기법** (형용사와 분사를 주격보어로 받는 동사)–분사는 be동사 제외

인생이 가고(go) 오고(come) 죽고(die) 산다(live)는 말이 무슨 소리인가(sound).
　인생은 잠시 나타나(appear) 머물며(stay) 앉고(sit) 서다(stand)를 반복하다 영원히 남아있지(remain) 못하고 떨어져(fall) 달아나버리는(run) 낙엽인 듯싶어라.(seem)
　어릴 땐 엄마 품에 편히 누워(lie) 있다가(be) 자라서는(grow) 결혼도 하고(marry) 재물도 얻고(get) 성공도 만들어(make) 지키려고(keep) 애쓰다가 갑자기 쫓아내듯(turn out) 세상 밖으로 나오게 되니(come out) 이 어찌 인생의 쓴맛(taste)과 고통의 냄새(smell)를 느끼지(feel) 않게 되리요(become).
　보라(look) 돌아가(turn) 하나님의 자녀로 증명(prove) 되지 못하면 얼마나 허망한가?

I stood reading the book.

He sat reading the book.

He sat surrounded by the crowd.

4) be 동사 + to 부정사

C

My policy is to wait and see

5) be 동사 + 동명사

          C

My hobby is collecting stamps. → 동명사로 보어이다

I'm collecting stamps. → 현재진행형 동사

6) be 동사 + 절보어

          C

The trouble is [that my father is ill in bed].

                       절 보어

This is [what I like to do].

          절 보어

1. She wants go to Italy.

2. She denied have stolen anything.

3. You must not postpone answer her letter any longer.

4. We agreed start early.

5. He learned drive a car.

6. I refused discuss the question.

7. I don't choose be a candidate.

8. The boy decided become a sailor.

9. He never fails write to his mother every week.

10. I don't mind smoke here.

11. We desire say something.

12. She longed say something.

13. He asked to see the paper.

14. They enjoyed drive on the new highway.

15. We're planning visit Africa this summer.

16. He never misses go to church every Sunday.

17. He determined learn Greek.

18. She wishes be alone.

19. I expect be back on Sunday.

20. We hope see you soon.

21. He is considering go with his mother.

22. She wants me go with her.

23. Do you really want me go?

24. She expects her husband return.

25. He attempted solve a problem.

26. The boss demanded know what's going on.

27. Don't forget post the letter.

28. He has finished do his homework.

29. I asked him do that.

30. Allow me introduce my friend to you .

31. I couldn't force myself sleep.

32. The doctor ordered the patient take a long rest.

33. Good health enables him carry out the plan.

34. I forced him not use that word.

35. I want you come here tomorrow.

36. He ordered me do this work.

37. He didn't see me left there all alone.

38. You heard him to go out.

39. I watched him to across the street.

40. I help him found his thing.

1. The spacious room has much furniture.

2. Much clothing is needed in cold countries.

3. To tell him directly will make him angry.

4. She was a mother of three children.

5. To use a bag only once is a waste.

6. Water is composed of oxygen and hydrogen.

7. Asking him the question will be a waste of time.

8. To be always on time is the duty of a gentleman.

9. The water in this glass is not good to drink.

10. The milk in the bottle went bad.

11. The beauty of the scenery is beyond description.

12. To eat too much is bad for the health.

always	부) 늘, 언제나, 항상	angry	형) 노한, 성난
ask	동) ~을 묻다. 부탁하다		
bad	형) 나쁜, 불량한 go bad -(음식 등이)상하다		
bag	명) 가방	beauty	명) 아름다움, 미
beyond	전) ~의 저쪽에, 너머에, ~보다나은	bottle	명) 병
child	명) 어린이 복수 - children	clothing	명) 의복, 의류
cold	형) 추운, 찬		
compose	동) ~을 구성하다, ~의 일부를 이루다 (be composed of~; ~으로 이루어지다)		
country	명) 나라, 지방 복수–countries	description	명) 서술, 기술, 해설
directly	부) 직접적으로, 똑바로, 바로	drink	동) 마시다
duty	명) 의무, 책임, 도의	eat	동) 먹다
furniture	명) 가구	gentleman	명) 신사
glass	명) 유리	good	형) 좋은, 훌륭한
health	명) 건강	him	(he의 목적격) 그를, 그에게
hydrogen	명) 수소(원소 중 제일 가벼운 기체)	make	동) 만들다, 야기하다, 시키다, 되다
mother	명) 어머니, 모친	much	형) (양이) 많은
need	동) ~을 필요로 하다	once	부) 한번, 일찍이, 한때
only	부) 오직, 단지	oxygen	명) 산소
question	명) 질문	room	명) 방, 실(室)
scenery	명) 풍경, 경관, 경치	spacious	형) 넓은, 거대한, (도량이)넓은
tell	동) ~을 말하다, 알리다	time	명) 시간, 때, 세월 on time - 정각에
too	부) 매우, 또한, 게다가	use	동) ~를 사용하다, 이용하다
waste	명) 낭비, 동)~을 낭비하다, 허비하다	water	명) 물
will	(미래시제조동사)~일 것이다		

13 ¹In the beginning God created the heavens and the earth. ²The earth was empty, a formless mass cloaked in darkness. And the Spirit of God was hovering over its surface. (Genesis 1:1~2)

14. ¹So the creation of the heavens and the earth and everything in them was completed. ²On the seventh day, having finished his task, God rested from all his work. ³And God blessed the

seventh day and declared it holy, because it was the day when he rested from his work of creation. ⁴This is the account of the creation of the heavens and the earth. When the LORD God made the heavens and the earth, ⁵there were no plants or grain growing on the earth, for the LORD God had not sent any rain. And no one was there to cultivate the soil. ⁶But water came up out of the ground and watered all the land. ⁷And the LORD God formed a man's body from the dust of the ground and breathed into it the breath of life. And the man became a living person. ⁸Then the LORD God planted a garden in Eden, in the east, and there he placed the man he had created. ⁹And the LORD God planted all sorts of trees in the garden—beautiful trees that produced delicious fruit. At the center of the garden he placed the tree of life and the tree of the knowledge of good and evil. ¹⁰A river flowed from the land of Eden, watering the garden and then dividing into four branches. ¹¹One of these branches is the Pishon, which flows around the entire land of Havilah, where gold is found. (Genesis 2:1~11)

15. ¹In the beginning the Word already existed. He was with God, and he was God. ²He was in the beginning with God. ³He created everything there is. Nothing exists that he didn't make. ⁴Life itself was in him, and this life gives light to everyone. ⁵The light shines through the darkness, and the darkness can never extinguish it. ⁶God sent John the

Baptist [7]to tell everyone about the light so that everyone might believe because of his testimony. [8]John himself was not the light; he was only a witness to the light. [9]The one who is the true light, who gives light to everyone, was going to come into the world. (John 1:1~9)

♠단어학습♠

account	명) 설명, 보고	all	형) 전부의, 내내의, 모든
already	부) 이미, 벌써	any	형) 무슨, 조금도
baptist	명) 침례(세례)주는 사람	beautiful	형)아름다운
become	동) ~이 되다, 일어나다		
beginning	명) 시초, 최초 in the beginning-태초에		
believe	동) 믿다	body	명) 몸, 육체
branch	명) 가지, 부문		
breathe	동) 숨쉬다, ~into;~에게 새 생명을 불어넣다		
center	명) 중심, 중앙		
cloak	동) (~ in) ~으로 덮다, ~을 은폐하다		
come up	동) 떠오르다	complete	형) 완성된, 철저한, 동) ~을 완성하다
create	동) ~을 창조하다, ~을 만들어 내다	cultivate	동) ~을 갈다, 경작하다, 재배하다
darkness	명) 어둠	delicious	형) 맛있는
divide	동) 나누다 ~into ☆ ~을 ☆로 나누다		
dust	명) 먼지	earth	명) (the ~) -땅, 지상, 대지, 육지
east	명) 동쪽	empty	형) 빈, 아무도 없는
entire	형) 전체의, 완전한	everyone	대) 누구든지, 모두
everything	대) 모든 것	evil	명) 악, 악의 형) 나쁜, 악질의
exist	동) 존재하다, 실재하다	extinguish	동) (불을)끄다, 소멸시키다
finish	동) ~을 끝내다, 종결하다	flow	동) 흐르다, 순환하다
form	동) 형성하다	formless	형) 모양이 없는, 실체가 없는
fruit	명) 과일	garden	명) 정원
give	동) ~을 주다	God	명) 신, 하나님, 창조주
gold	명) 금	good	명) 좋은 것, 선 형)좋은, 충분한
grain	명) 곡식알, 낱알	ground	명) 땅
grow	동) 자라다, 발육하다	heaven	명) 하늘, 천국 (보통 the heavens)
hover	동) 공중을 날다, 빙빙 맴돌다 (~over)	itself	대) 그 자신, 바로그것
knowledge	명) 지식, 학문	land	명) 뭍, 육지
life	명) 생명, 삶	mass	명) 덩어리

no	아니오	nothing	대) 아무것도 ~아니다 명)무
place	명) 장소, 동) ~을 놓다, 배치하다	plant	명) 식물 동)~ (씨)를 뿌리다
produce	동) ~을 제조하다, 생산하다	rain	명) 비, 동) 비가 내리다
rest	동) 쉬다, 명) 휴식	river	명) 강,하천
send	동) 보내다	shine	동) 빛나다, 밝게 빛나다
soil	명) 흙, 토양	sort	명) 종류, 품종
spirit	명) 정신, 영혼	surface	명) 표면, 외면, 외관
task	명) 일, 직무	testimony	명) 증언, 증거, 증명
them	대) ((they의 목적격)) 그들을, 그것들을		
there	부) 거기에, (be동사와 함께 존재) 있다		
through	전) ~을 통과하여,~을 통하여	true	형) 참된, 진실의
water	명) 물	witness	명) 목격자, 증인
word	명) 말, 언어	work	명) 일, 노동, 공부 동) 일하다, 작업하다

Amazing Predictions for the Future

Everyone wonders what the future will bring. In your great-grandchildren's lifetime, dinner might be served by robots, and airplanes might fly without pilots. Who knows? Maybe we won't even need airplanes to fly from place to place.

Our vision of the future keeps changing. At your age, your great-grandparents never dreamed that personal computers would receive e-mail letters from anywhere in the world. In the same way, tomorrow's wonders are probably beyond our imagination. Even so, it's fun to try to guess what the future will bring.

COMPUTER-WEAR

In the future, messages from a portable computer may appear

on an eyeglass lens. Also, eyeglasses with a camera and speaker in them may whisper into your ear the name of the person you're facing – in case you've forgotten it. Even clothes will be smart. High-tech clothes will warm or cool you any time you want.

VIDEO WRISTWATCHES

In the future, you'll be able to phone home with video wristwatches. At the touch of a button, you'll talk to people across the street or even across the ocean. Smile! A video image of your face will be sent along with your voice.

VIRTUAL REALITY

Suppose you are stuck in the house. Don't be sad. You'll slip on a virtual reality (VR) helmet and enjoy a virtual party with your friends on a computer. You might use a VR helmet to play along inside a television game show, join your favorite rock band onstage, or leap into an action film. The future will be bright for couch potatoes!

DOOR-TO-DOOR DRIVERLESS TAXIS

No cars in the future? No problem! At a taxi station, you'll simply say your destination into a voice-recognition machine. A door will open to a small, automated taxi as the fare is electronically paid from your bank account. Then the taxi will take you to your destination.

MIRACLE CHIPS

"Billy? Where are you?" When a child gets lost, the parents will find him or her without difficulty. Every child will carry a microchip, and it will help the parents to find them. The same kind of chip could also serve as a library card, driver's license, and medical record.

Wonders in the future are probably beyond our imagination. "We study the future so we can prepare for tomorrow," explains Joseph Coates, a futurist from Washington, D.C. Futurists help companies and governments plan ahead – but not too far ahead. Technology is changing quickly, so predictions that look beyond the next 30 years would be mostly guesswork. "Looking into the future is an art, not a science," says Coates.

♣단어학습♣

account	명) 계좌	across	전) ~을 가로질러, 횡단하여
ahead	부) 앞쪽에, 앞으로	airplane	명) 비행기
amazing	형) 놀랄만한	anywhere	부) 어디든지 명) 어딘가
appear	동) 나타나다	art	명) 예술
automate	동) ~을 자동화하다	bring	동) ~을 가져오다, 초래하다
carry	동) ~을 운반하다	chairman	명) 의장, 사회자, 회장
chip	명) 칩, 반도체 소자	company	명) 친구, 동료, 회사
deal	동) 대처하다, 처리하다, 논하다 (~with)		
destination	명) 목적지, 행선지	difficulty	명) 어려움, 곤란
dream	명) 꿈, 동) 꿈을 꾸다	driver	명) 운전자

electronically	형) 전자의, 온라인의	explain	동) 설명하다
eyeglass	명) 외알안경, 접안렌즈	face	동) 마주대하다, 직면하다 명) 얼굴
fare	명) 요금, 운임	fly	동) 날다
forget	동) 잊다 과거-forgot	futurist	명) 미래신자, 인류 진보의 신봉자
government	명) 정부		
grandchild	명) 손자, 손녀 복) grandchildren		
guess	동) 추측하다	guesswork	명) 어림짐작
high-tech	명) 첨단기술	imagination	명) 상상
issue	명) 공포, 발행, 쟁점	library	명) 도서관, 문고
license	명) 자격증	lifetime	명) 일생, 생애
lost	형) 잃어버린, lose의 과거형-잃다	medical	형) 의학의, 의술의
message	명) 알림, 통지, 메시지	miracle	명) 기적, 신기
mostly	부) 대부분의, 주로	next	형) 다음의
ocean	명) 대양, 해양, 바다	pay	동) 지불하다
personal	형) 개인의, 사적인, 개인용의	plan	동) 계획하다
portable	형) 휴대용의, 간편한	prediction	명) 예언, 예보
prepare	동) 준비하다	press	동) ～을 누르다, 밀어 붙이다.
probably	부) 아마도	quickly	부) 빨리
receive	동) 받다	record	명) 기록 동) ～을 기록하다
replace	동) ～을 대신하다, 제자리에 놓다	ruling	명) 지배, 통치 형) 지배하는, 유력한
sad	형) 슬픈	serve	동) ～에 봉사하다,(음식 등을) 제공하다
simply	부) 간단히, 간편하게	slip	동) 미끄러지다
smart	형) 영리한, 빈틈없는	strike	동) ～을 가하다, 공격하다
study	동) 공부하다	suppose	동) ～이라 가정하다, 상상하다
technology	명) 기술	vision	명) 시력, 환상, 통찰력, 미래상
warm	형) 따뜻한	whisper	동) 속삭이다, 밀담하다 명) 속삭임
without	부) 없이	wristwatch	명) 손목시계

♣단어학습♣

science	명)과학	escape	동)달아나다, 탈출하다
ask	동)묻다, 요청하다	yourself	대)당신자신
purpose	명)목적, 용도, 의도	express	동)표현하다
own	형)자기소유의	feeling	명)촉감, 감각
write	동)～을쓰다	fact	명)사실
information	명)정보	persuade	동)설득하다
mind	명)마음	subject	명)주제, 화제
each	형)각자의, 각각의	first	형)최초의, 첫번째의
pack	명)꾸러미, 짐 동)짐을 꾸리다, 싸다	trick	명)책략, 계략, 속임수

wave	명)파도,물결, (손)흔들기, 동)손을흔들다	scratch	동)긁다, 할퀴다
stand	동)서다, 서있다	zookeeper	명)(동물원)사육사
bath	명)목욕	cage	명)새장, 우리
promise	명)약속, 계약 동)약속하다	soccer	명)축구
article	명)기사, 논설	newspaper	명)신문
reward	명)보수, 보상,		

official	명)공무원, 관리	offer	동)~을 제공하다
spider	명)거미, 거미같은것	brown	명)갈색, 밤색
weigh	동)저울에 달다. ~을 평가하다	ounce	명)온스 (무게의 단위)
director	명)지도자, 지휘자	capture	동)~을 붙잡다, 체포하다
special	형)특별한	handler	명)다루는 사람
available	형)쓸모있는, 유용한	councilman	명)(지방의회의)의원, 평의원

remind	동)~을 상기시키다	guard	동)지키다, 보호하다
patrol	동)순회하다, 순찰하다	protection	명)보호
second	형)두번째의	urge	동)재촉하다, 주장하다
vote	명)투표, ~을 투표로 결정하다	provide	동)제공하다

Bomba Escapes from the Zoo

When you are writing, ask yourself what your purpose is. Are you writing simply to express your own feelings? Are you writing to give facts and other kinds of information? Are you writing to persuade other people to change their minds about something? The writings that follow are about the same subject. But each has a different purpose. As you read, think about how differently the subject is presented for each purpose.

I will never forget the first time I saw Bomba the monkey at the Evanstown Zoo. It was a sunny Sunday afternoon. The place was packed with people watching the new monkey. I felt Bomba was doing all of his tricks just for me. If I waved at him, he waved at me. If I scratched my head, he scratched his head. An old man standing by me said, "Well, this monkey sure likes you!"

I never did go to see the zookeepers giving the baby elephant a bath. Instead, I stayed by the monkey cage for two or three hours. I felt sad to leave Bomba, and he seemed sorry to see me go. I promised him I'd be back soon.

Then I got busy with school work, soccer, and all kinds of other things. I was planning to go to see Bomba again this weekend. But now an article in the newspaper says Bomba escaped yesterday. There's a big reward for giving information about Bomba. I don't want any money. I just want Bomba to be back safely in his cage.

[2]

MONKEY ESCAPES FROM ZOO

A monkey escaped from the Evanstown Zoo yesterday. Zoo officials are offering a $1,000 reward for information.

The spider monkey, known as Bomba, is brown and weighs ten pounds nine ounces. It was born in the zoo and has always lived there.

Andrea Coleman, Director of the Zoo, asks the public not to try to capture the monkey. For the safety of the public and the monkey, special animal handlers will be available 24 hours a day. Anyone having any information about the missing monkey is asked to call Ms. Coleman at the special Missing Animals Hot Line,555-ZOOS.

[3]

Dear Town Councilman Smith:

The escape of Bomba the monkey from the Evanstown Zoo reminds us that we need more guards at the zoo. Because of outs in funding, the number of zoo guards has been cut in half. Instead of two guards patrolling the zoo grounds, there is now only one. There are two reasons to keep two guards on duty at all times. The first reason is for the safety and protection of the animals in the zoo. The second reason is for the safety and protection of the public. I urge you to vote "yes" on the bill that will provide more funding for the zoo.

♣단어학습♣

stressful	형)긴장(스트레스)이 많은	natural	형)자연의,천연의,타고난,당연한
necessary	형)필요한, 없어서는 안될	recognize	동)~을보고 곧 알아보다, ~을 인식하다
weakness	명)약함, 허약	behavior	명)행동, 행위, 처신, 행실
often	부)몹시,자주	comfortable	형)쾌적한, 안락한, 편안한
easy	형)쉬운, 용이한	stay	동)머무르다
give up	동)포기하다, 그만두다	old	형)오래된, 늙은
comfort	동)~을위로하다, 격려하다 명)위로,위안	habit	명)버릇
wonder	명)놀랄만한 것, 경이 동) 이상하게여기다	dislike	동)싫어하다

Growing as a person may take you to new places and present new challenges. These may be stressful, but feeling stress is a natural, necessary part of recognizing a weakness and trying out a new behavior. It is often comfortable and easy to stay the way we are. Giving up old comforts and habits is very hard. It is small wonder that people dislike changing. (수능기출문제)

♣단어학습♣

foreigner	명)외국사람	steady	형)확고한, 튼튼한
progress	명)전진, 진행 동)나아가다, 전진하다	university	명)대학
program	명)프로그램, 계획, 스케줄	abroad	부)해외에, 외국으로
textbook	명)교과서	learner	명)학습자
benefit	명)이익 동)~에게 이익이 되다	worker	명)일(공부)하는 사람
coworker	명)협력자	volunteer	명)자원봉사자
establish	동)~을 수립하다	educational	형)교육상의, 교육적인

Since the mid-1990s, teaching Korean to foreigners has made quiet and steady progress. Many universities now offer Korean language programs in Korea and abroad, and many textbooks have been produced for learners of Korean. Only a small number of foreigners, however, have benefited from this progress. Most foreign workers are being taught by Korean co-workers or volunteers who have no or little teaching experience. Thus, it is necessary to establish better educational programs for teaching the Korean language to foreign workers. (수능기출문제)

♣단어학습♣

by no, means	결코 ~ 않은	well off	부유한
rush	동)돌진하다, 갑자기 달려들다 형)바쁜	last	형)최후의, 마지막의
attempt	동)시도하다, 꾀하다 명)시도	catch up	따라잡다

identical	형)똑같은, 동일한	greeting	명)인사, 절
snap	동)찰깍하고 소리나다 (~up)을잡아채다	sign	명)표, 기호
post	동)우송하다sigh명)한숨 동)한숨쉬다,탄식하다	sigh	명)한숨 동)한숨쉬다, 탄식하다
relief	명)제거, 경감	gift	명)선물

There was a kind woman who made a last attempt to catch up. Seeing a box of 50 identical greeting cards in a shop, she snapped it up, carried it home, and signed 49 cards before midnight. She posted them the next morning and gave a sigh of relief. Then she opened one remaining card, and found these words printed on it : This little card is just to say a gift from me is on the way.(수능기출문제)

♣단어학습♣

supervise	동)감독하다	warehouse	명)창고
offer	동)제공하다	operation	명)작업, 조작
base on	~에 기초를 두다	frequent	형) 자주 일어나는, 빈번한
responsibility	명)책임감	record	명)기록, 동) 기록하다
prove	동)증명하다		

Thomas Jefferson once said that what matters is the courage of one's convictions. Do you have the courage which comes from the sincere conviction that you are a person of sound character, an honest, dependable, kind, and caring person ? If you do, you will never have to worry about what others think of you. If you know in your heart that you are a good anddecent Person, you can life's challenges head-on and without fear of what others think.
(수능기출문제)

♣단어학습♣

approach   접근하다   intersection   교차로 즉시 의식 방향

wheelchair   휠체어   costly lesson   값비싼 교훈

A terrible accident changed my life. A friend and I were driving home from a midnight movie. As we approached an intersection, we stopped at a red light. No cars seemed to be coming, so I decided to go through the red light. Immediately after we started, I lost consciousness. Later I learned that we had hit a car coming from the other direction. That accident made my friend spend the rest of his life in a wheelchair, and I learned a costly lesson.(수능기출문제)

-고급 문장-

1. As the tadpole grows older the cells composing its tail are attacked and absorbed by certain body cells until the tail shrinks and finally disappears completely.[사법고시]

♣단어학습♣

· tadpole : 올챙이   · cell : 세포

· absorb : 흡수하다   · shrink : 줄어들다   · resume : 되찾다.

2. During the American Revolution the people of Canada remained loyal to England although the rebelling colonies tried to persuade them to join the war for independence. [한국전력]

♣단어학습♣

· revolution : 혁명　　　　　　　· loyal : 충성의
· rebel : 항거하다　　　　　　　· colony : 거류민
· persuade : 설득하다　　　　　· surrender : 항복하다

3. The Korean economic system does not exist in isolation but is a part of the world-wide economic system. Thus, the economic life of the Korean people is greatly affected by the economic life of all the peoples. [사법고시]

♣단어학습♣

· exist : 존재하다　　　　· isolation : 고립
· affect : 영향을 끼치다　　· product : 농산물　　　· stock market : 증권시장

4. Today, our enormous investment in science and research is the evidence of our faith that science can not only make man richer but it can make man better. [포항공대 대학원]

♣단어학습♣

· enormous : 막대한　　　· investment : 투자
· research : 연구　　　　· evidence : 증거

5. But in 1799 an officer in Napoleon's army discovered near the Egyptian village of Rosetta a smooth, thick black stone covered with carvings that were divided into three separate sections. [TOEFL]

♣단어학습♣

· officer : 장교　　　　· carvings : 조각
· separate : 분리된　　　· section : 부분

6. In northern countries many insects and worms that cannot live in winter die when cold weather comes. They leave larvae, or egg, to revive their species the following spring. [행정고시]]

♠단어학습♠
· worm : 벌레   · larvae : 유충
· revive : 소생시키다   · species : 종, 종류

7. The animal's mouth is disproportionately large in comparison with his narrow throat. When he fills his mouth with food, he must chew for a long time before he can swallow. [한국외대 대학원, 행정고시]

♠단어학습♠
· disproportionately : 어울리지 않게   · in comparison with : ～와 비교해서
· throat : 목구멍   · gnaw : 갉아먹다   · swallow : 삼키다

8. If democracy is to survive ,above all the thing that a teacher should endeavor to produce in his pupils is the kind of tolerance that springs from an endeavor to understand those who are different from ourselves. [한양대 대학원]

♠단어학습♠
· democracy : 민주주의   · survive : 살아남다
· above all : 특히, 우선   · endeavor : 노력, 노력하다
· tolerance : 아량, 관용   · spring from : ～에서 생기다

9. Just when many of the nation's contractors were looking into moving out of the industry, the unfortunate result of the earthquake has created an enormous demand for construction. [TOEIC]

♣단어학습♣

· enormous : 엄청난 · contractor : 토건업자, 도급업자
· look into : 조사하다 · demand : 수요

10. Drama thrived in India a long time ago, and since the plays presented there always had happy endings, Hindu theatergoers were strangers to tragedies. [외무고시]

♣단어학습♣

· thrive : 번창하다 · theatergoer : 관객
· tragedy : 비극 · costume : 의복

구(Phrase)와 절(Clause)을 찾는 공식

우리는 앞 과정을 통해서 문장의 핵심 요소인 주어, 동사, 목적어, 보어를 찾는 방법과 문장의 다양한 예문을 통해 문장의 내용을 쉽게 파악하는 훈련을 하였다.

*구 : 둘 이상의 단어가 모여 하나의 문장 요소, 즉 주어, 동사, 목적어, 보어, 수식어의 기능을 하는 단어 집단으로서「주어+동사」를 포함하지 않은 것이다.

1. 구의 구성

영어에서는 구가 될 수 있는 것이 다음 세 가지가 있다.
① 전치사 + 명사 · · · · · ·전명구
② to + 원형 · · · · · · · ·부정사구
③ 분사 · · · · · · · · ·분사구

2.형용사구 – 부정사구, 전명구, 분사구

1) 부정사구

In my hometown **to grow**, I had a dream for the future.

I have no book **to read**.

He has many children **to look after**.

※ 명사를 수식하는 부정사와 전치사
　　Something **to write** (쓸 대상)
　　Something **to write with** (쓸 도구)
　　Something **to write on** (쓸 종이)
　　Something **to write about** (쓸 제목)
　　a house **to live in** (살 집)
　　a some money **to live on** (살아갈 돈)

The ability **to use** good English is enhanced by careful observation of distinctions between uses of synonyms.

2) 전명구 (형태 : 명사 + 전명구)

By a strange combination **of generosity** and greed man protects

                          형용사구

the weak **in asylums** /and/ kills the strong **in wars**.

In 1799 an officer **in Napoleon's army** discovered a smooth,

                      형용사구

thick, black stone.

A major step **in the development of jazz** was taken by musicians.

        형용사구   형용사구

3) 분사구

In the book **written** in Ratin, I found a mystery of devil.

       과거 분사구

The soldiers **wounded** in the battle were sent to the hospital.

       과거 분사구

The man **speaking** to the mayor is my uncle.

I received a letter **written** in English.

       과거분사구

<u>It</u>　is <u>difficult</u>　to study animals **living** under water.

현재분사구

※ 수동의 의미일 때 과거 분사, 능동의 의미일 때 현재분사를 사용한다.

*절 : 「주어+동사」를 갖추어 문장 형태를 이루고 있다. 문장 내에서 명사, 형용사, 부사 등의 구실을 하는 구문으로서 문장 가운데 포함된 「작은 문장」이라고 할 수 있다.

1. 형용사절

문장 내에서 **명사를 수식하는 형용사적 역할**을 하는 절로서 관계대명사절이나 관계부사절이 이에 속한다. 형용사절은 **절 전체가 명사를 수식한**다. 형용사절을 만드는 단어는 **모두 10개**가 있다.

> ● 관계대명사 : Who, whose, whom, which, that
> ● 관계부사　: When, where, why, how, that

(1) 형용사절

격 선행사	주격	소유격	목적격
사람	who	whose	whom
동물, 사물	which	whose(=of which)	which
사람, 동물, 사물	that	–	that

1) 관계대명사 : who, whose, whom, which, that

☞ This is the girl [who is a good typist].

This is the boy [whom I wanted to see].

A child [whose parents are dead] is called an orphan.

I employed a man [whom I thought to be honest].

I have a book [which is very interesting].

This is the dictionary [which I bought yesterday].

Mt. Everest is the mountain [of which the top is covered
with snow].   = [whose top is covered with snow].

A man and his dogs [that were passing by]were injured].
　　사람 + 동물

He is the greatest poet [that Korea has ever produced].
　　　　최상급

This is the last money [that you shall ever receive].
　　the last + 명사

He is the only man [that I can trust].

    the only + 명사

You are the very boy [that I have been looking for].

    the very + 명사

that의 주의해야 할 용법
명사절에 계속적인 용법에 쓰일 수 없고 형용사절에서 소유격에 사용할 수 없다.

2. 관계부사

1) 시간+ when+S+V+★

2) 장소+ where+S+V+★

3) 이유+ why+S+V+★

4) 방법+ how+S+V+★

관계부사 다음에는 완전한 문장이 온다. (관계부사 + S + V)

This is the building **where** I work.

Do you remember that holiday **when** it rained everyday?

I don't know (the reason) **why** he went home.

This is (the way) **how** he did it.

* 일반적으로 the way와 how는 함께 쓰지 않는다.

♣ 관계부사 when, where는 앞의 명사를 선행사로 받을 수 있다.

☞ The hammer has been as a tool since the Neolithic Period, **when** it was invented.

☞ The Oregon Trail went through the South Pass, **where** gold was discovered in 1842.

*부사구 : 부사적 의미를 갖고 동사, 형용사, 다른 부사, 또는 문장 전체를 수식하는 단어집단을 말한다.   전명구, 부정사구, 분사구(문)

1. 전명구(전치사+명사)

In the North Atlantic and North Pacific Ocean all hurricanes are now given
전명구
girl's names. Many of the basic principles of biology have been discovered **by observation and experiment** with single cells.

* 명사+전명구로 전명구가 일반적으로 "~의, ~한"으로 해석이 되면 형용사구가 되고 다른 것으로 해석이 되면 부사구이다.

He has done it **with ease**.

(그는 그 일을 쉽게 해냈다.)

There is a white building **on the hill**.

(언덕 위에 흰색 건물이 하나 있다.)

2. 부정사구

1) <u>**To master**</u> the English language thoroughly and, consequently,
　　to부정사구

　to appreciate literature, a clear understanding <u>of the</u>
　　　to부정사구

　<u>Englishman's character</u> is <u>necessary</u>.

2) 일반동사 + to부정사 목적(부사구) "~하기 위해"

　We eat <u>**to live**</u>, not live <u>**to eat**</u>.
　　　to부정사구

　I got up early <u>**to catch**</u> the train.
　　　to부정사구

　He went abroad <u>**to study**</u> economics.
　　　to부정사구

3) 일반동사(~하니, ~해서) + to부정사 결과(동사로 해석)
　이때 동사가 awake, grow up 이 된다.

그리고 only to~ (~했으나 결국 ~하고 말았다)

    never to~ (~했으나 ~하지 못했다)

He awoke **to find** himself famous.

    to부정사구

He grow up **to be** a doctor.

    to부정사구

He did his best only **to fail** in the exam.

    to부정사구

He went to America never **to return**.

        to부정사구

4) 일반동사 + to부정사 원인 (부사구) "~하니까, ~하고나서"

    이때 감정 동사 ; smile, weep, rejoice…

        감정 형용사 happy, sad, sorry…

        감정 동사+ to부정사 원인(부사구)

        be동사 + 감정 형용사 + to부정사 원인(부사구)

He smiled **to see** the monkey.

        to부정사구

He wept **to see** the sight.

    to부정사구

I am glad **to meet** you.

　　to부정사구

I rejoice **to hear** of your success.

　　to부정사구

She was very happy **to get** the birthday present.

　　to부정사구

I am sorry **to give** you trouble.

　　to부정사구

5) 형용사+ to부정사 "정도"(부사구) : "to 이하 하기에 ~하다."

This book is too difficult **to read**.

　　to부정사구

You are too young **to marry**.

　　to부정사구

6) to 부정사 조건 (부사구)

To tell a lie again, you will be punished.

to부정사구

= If you tell a lie again, you will be punished.

3. 분사구문

분사구문으로 만들 수 있다.

부사절 단어 + S + V + ★, S + V + ★(부사절 S와 주절 S가 같은 경우)

– V+ing + ★, S + V + ★

◈ 분사구문으로 바꾸기

When he saw me, he ran away.

→ Seeing me, he ran away.

While I walked along the street, I met a friend of mine.

→ Walking along the street, I met a friend of mine.

*부사절

문장 내에서 부사의 역할을 하는 절로서 시간, 장소, 원인이나 이유, 목적, 결과, 조건, 양보 등의 의미를 갖는다. 부사절은 명사절과 형용사절에 비교할 때 광범위하며, 복잡, 다양하다. 공부하는 학생들이 부사절을 정복한다면 영어 구조학을 완성하는 것이며 어떤 문장도 자유롭게 해석할 수 있고 TOEFL, TOEIC, TEPS 등을 쉽게 정복할 수 있다.

〈부사절의 형태〉

부사절 단어 + S + V + ★, S + V + ★

(*때때로 S +V + ★, 부사절단어 + S + V + ★ 형태로 바뀔 수 있다.)

1. 시간 부사절

as(~할 때), since(~한 이래), when(~할 때), whenever(~어느 때든지), while(~하는 동안), after(~후에), before(전에), till=until(까지), as long as(하는 동안), as soon as(하자마자), the moment(곧)

<u>Whenever</u> they get right answers, the teacher praises the students.

You couldn't turn the heat off <u>so long as</u> the system was operating.

<u>As soon as</u> baby turtle is hatched, it must be able to fend for itself.

<u>When</u> the work of production is separated into occupation, glucose does not have to be digested.

Dried leaves continue to hang on the branches of some trees, <u>until</u> the new leaves appear.

I will try to finish this work, <u>before</u> you can come.

2. 장소 부사절

wherever(어디서~하여도) where

Sit <u>where</u> you like.

<u>Wherever</u> you go, I go too.

<u>Wherever</u> he is, he must be found.

3. 원인 · 이유 부사절

as(~하므로), since(~하므로), because(왜냐하면), now that(이제 ~이니까, ~인 이상), seeing that(~을 보니)

<u>Since</u> it was Saturday, he stayed in bed an extra hour.

<u>As</u> he had worked up since 4 a.m., he was no doubt now very tired.

<u>Now that</u> she found him, she'll never let him go.

<u>Seeing that</u> you're the guest on this little trip, you can decide where we're going.

◆ 분사구문으로 변형

As I have no money, I can't help you.
  → Having no money, I can't help you.

Since I feel tired, I will stay at home.
  → Feeling tired, I will stay at home.

4. 조건 부사절

if(~한다면), unless(~하지 않는다면), in case(that)(~하는 경우에), so long as (~하기만 하면), once (일단 ~하면), providing, provided(that), supposing(만약~한다면)

Take your coat in case it rains.

Our profits will be good, so long as the dollar remains strong.

Once she arrives, we can start.

So far as I know, they're coming by car.
If you turn to the right, you will find the house.

If a boxer is knocked down and can not rise within ten seconds, he loses the match.

I will come <u>provided(that)</u> it is fine tomorrow.

= providing

<u>Supposing</u> your father knew it, what would he say?

◆ 분사구문으로 변형

  <u>If you take this train</u>, you will arrive in London at six.

  → Taking this train, you will arrive in London at six.

5. 양보 부사절

although, (even)though(~일지라도), whether~or~(~인지 ~인지), 의문사(what, who, whose, whom, which..)+ever = no matter+의문사(what, who, whose, whom, which..)+(S)+may +V

Even though it's hard work, I enjoy it.

We'll go **even if** it rains.

Although Laurie has no formal training in computer science, she knows a great deal about computers.

Whatever I suggest, he always disagrees.

= **No matter what I may suggest**, he always disagrees.

◆ 분사구문으로 변형

  Though I admit what you say, I still don't believe it.

→ **Admitting** what you say, I still don't believe it.

Even if we grant that it is true, we can't agree with you.
→ **Granting** that it is true, we can't agree with you.

6. 목적 부사절

that~may, so that~may, in order that~may(~하기 위해)
lest~should, for fear that~should(~하지 않도록 하기 위해)

He works hard **so that** he **may** pass the exam.
               = **in order that~may**
               = **that~may**

Be careful **lest** you **should** fall from the tree.
  = Be careful **for fear that** you **should** fall from the tree.

7. 결과 부사절

so ~ that, such ~ that(너무~해서~하다), ~, so that~(~해서,~하다)
I was **so** hungry **that** I could not walk.

She told me to go, **so that** I went.

8. 양태, 비율 부사절

as(~처럼), as~so(~처럼, 그렇게),

As he grew disheartened, **so** his work deteriorated.

Two is to four **as** eight is to sixteen. (2:4=8:16).

9. 비교 부사절

than(~보다) → 종속절에서 <u>주절과 공통된 부분</u>이 생략될 수 있다.

She is brighter **than** her brother(is bright).

She respected him more **than I** (**than I** respected him).

구분

she respected him more than me(than은 전치사)

10. whereas : 반면에 (문장 중간에 온다) = while

Humans are capable of making errors **whereas** the computer
is not.

준동사

준동사: 1) 동명사, 2) to부정사, 3) 분사

동사의 의미만을 가지고 있을 뿐 동사의 수, 시제는 없기 때문에 절대로 **술어동사가 될 수 없다**. 준동사는 **주어, 목적어, 보어, 형용사구, 부사구 역할을 함과 동시에 동사가 가지고 있는 모든 기능을 다 한다**. 준동사 때문에 문장이 복잡해지고 길어진다. 그러므로 준동사를 정확한 이해가 필요하다.

– 분사 준동사 –

That girl <u>wearing</u> a big red hat is my sister.
(큰 빨간 모자를 쓰고 있는 저 소녀는 나의 동생이다)

The boy <u>sleeping</u> in the sun is my brother.
(양지에서 자고 있는 소년은 나의 남동생이다)

I like the friend <u>lending</u> me many books.
(나에게 많은 책을 빌려준 그 친구를 좋아한다).

Tom has a beautiful sister <u>called</u> as Bessy.
(팀은 베시라고 불려지는 아름다운 여동생이 있다)
My father had a large house **built** of red stone.
(나의 아버지는 빨간 돌로 세워진 큰 집이 있었다)

A letter **written** in English was delivered to me.
(영어로 쓴 한 통의 편지가 나에게 배달되었다)

- 동명사(동사원형 + ing) 준동사 -

Reading newspaper is very important.
(신문을 읽는 것은 매우 중요하다)

My work is **cleaning** the rooms.
(나의 일은 방을 청소하는 것이다)

I like **studying** English.
(나는 영어 공부하기를 좋아한다)

She went away without **saying** a word.
(그녀는 한 마디 말도 없이 나가 버렸다)

He insisted on **my paying** for bread.
(그는 나더러 빵값을 치르라고 강요했다)

She had no doubt of **her son('s) coming** back to her.
(그녀는 자기 아들이 돌아오리라는 것을 의심치 않았다)

He is proud of **his father('s) being** rich.
(그는 자기 아버지가 부자인 것을 자랑하고 있다)

* 현재분사(동사원형 + ing)와 동명사(동사원형 + ing)의 모양이 똑같으므로 구별하는
　방법은 놓이는 위치에 따라 달라진다.

① 동사원형 + ing가 현재분사로 쓰이는 경우
　동사원형 + ing 바로 앞에 명사가 있으면 동사원형 + ing는 현재분
　사로 바로 앞의 명사를 수식하여 주는 단어 수식요소로 쓰인다.

The boy **reading a** newspaper is my brother.

(신문을 읽고 있는 소년은 내 동생이다)

I do not like the work **cleaning** the room.

(나는 방을 청소하는 일을 싫어한다)

② 동사원형 + ing가 동명사로 쓰이는 경우

동사원형 + ing 바로 앞에 명사가 없으면 동사원형 + ing는 동명사로 명사 상당어구의 역할을 한다.

Reading newspaper is very important.

(신문을 읽는 것은 매우 중요하다)

My work is **cleaning** the rooms.

(나의 일은 방을 청소하는 것이다)

I like **studying** English.

(나는 영어 공부하기를 좋아한다)

She went away without **saying** a word.

(그녀는 한 마디 말도 없이 나가 버렸다)

– to부정사 준동사 –

부정사 준동사는 형용사구, 명사구, 부사구 모두 쓰인다. 각 역할을 함과 동시에 동사의 기능을 같이 한다.

<u>**To use**</u> the dictionary <u>is</u> <u>necessary</u>

Tom **to give** me money is kind

※ 준동사를 부정하는 방법 ※

준동사(현재분사, 과거분사, 동명사, to-부정사) 바로 앞에 not을 쓰면
된다.

My father told me not to go there.
(아버지는 나에게 그곳에 가지 말라고 말씀하셨다.)

I decided not to write a letter to my mother.
(나는 어머니께 편지를 쓰지 않기로 결심했다.)

Not being late for school is my habit.
(학교에 늦지 않는 것이 나의 습관이다.)

1. *B as well as A = A뿐만 아니라 B*

   This book is instructive **as well as** interesting.

   (이 책은 재미있을 뿐만 아니라 유익하다.)

2. *above ~ing = ~하지 않는*

   He's **above telling** lies.

   (그는 거짓말을 하지 않는다 = 그는 거짓말 따위를 할 사람이 아니다)

3. *all + 추상명사 추상명사 +itself = 매우 ~하다*

   He was **all kindness**. (= He was **kindness itself**.)

   (그는 매우 친절하다.)

4. *all the + 비교급 + for[because] ~ = ~ 때문에 더욱 좋다*

It is **all the better for** her beauty.

(= It is **all the better because** she's beautiful.)

(그녀는 미인이기 때문에 더욱 더 좋다.)

5. *as ~ as A = A만큼 ~ 한*

She is as tall **as** Mary.

(그녀는 메리만큼 키가 크다)

6. *as ~ as possible [주어 + can] = 가능한 한~하게*

He ran **as** fast **as** he could.

(= He ran **as** fast **as** possible.)

(그는 가능한 한 빨리 달렸다.)

7. *as ~ as any + ~ (명사) = ~ 못지 않게 ~하다*
   as ~ as ever + ~ (과거분사)~ = 지금까지 ~ 한사람 못지 않게 ~.
   하다(이다)

He works **as** hard **as any** student.

(그는 어느 학생 못지 않게 열심히 공부한다.)

He is **as** great a violinist **as ever** lived.

(그는 지금까지 있었던 누구 못지 않게 위대한 바이올린 연주가이다.)

8. *as~. so ~ = ~한만큼 ~하다*

As you sow, **so** will you reap.

(네가 씨를 뿌린 만큼 거둘 것이다.)

9. as it is = 있는 그대로 ; 실은

Leave the vase **as it is**.

(꽃병은 그대로 두십시오.)

If I were rich, I would buy a Cadillac, but **as it is**, I cannot buy a Ford.

(내게 만약 돈이 있다면 캐딜락을 사고 싶지만, 실은 포도도 살 수 없다.)

10. as many ∼ as ∼ = ∼하는 만큼 ∼을 ∼를 ∼만큼

You may pick **as many** flowers **as** you like.

(네가 원하는 만큼 꽃을 꺾어도 좋다.)

You must eat **as many** vegetables **as** meat.

(당신이 고기를 먹는 양만큼의 채소를 먹어야 한다.)

11. as much as ∼ = ∼만큼

Boys enjoyed the cartoons just **as much as** did girls.

(소년들은 소녀들이 즐겼던 만큼 만화영화를 즐겼다.)

12. between A and B∼ = A와 B 사이

The Middle East is located **between** India and Europe.

(중동은 인도와 유럽 사이에 위치하고 있다.)

13. both A and B = A와 B 둘다

He can **both** sing **and** dance.

(그는 노래도 할 수 있고 춤도 출 수 있다.)

14. buy A for B = pay B for A~ =B의 값을 치르고 A를 사다

I **bought** this bag **for** 5000 won.

(나는 5000원을 주고 이 가방을 샀다.)

15. cannot but + 동사원형 = cannot help ~ ing = ~하지 않을 수 없다

I **cannot but** admire him.

(나는 그에게 감탄하지 않을 수 없다.)

I **cannot help** admiring him.

(나는 그에게 감탄하지 않을 수 없다.)

16. compare A to B = A를 B에 비유하다

Man's life **is** often **compared to** a candle.

(사람의 생애는 종종 촛불에 비유된다.)

17. compare A with B = A를 B와 비교하다

Compare your pen **with** his.

(너의 펜을 그의 펜과 비교하라.)

18. either A or B = A 또는 B

Either he **or** his brother has to succeed to the business.

(그 또는 그의 형이 사업을 계승해야 한다.)

19. from A to B = A에서 B까지

Inho and I saw the film **from** the beginning **to** the end.

(인호와 나는 그 영화를 처음부터 끝까지 보았다.)

20. *have something to do with ~ = ~와 관계가 있다*

I **have** something **to do with** him.(평서문)

(나는 그와 관계가 있다.)

Have you anything **to do with** the matter?(의문문)

(당신은 그 일과 무슨 상관이 있습니까?)

I'll **have** nothing **to do with** such a fellow.(부정문)

(그런 인간과는 끝이다.)

21. *keep[prevent] A from ~ing =A가 ~ 하지 못하게 하다*

The rain **kept** me **from** *going* there.

(비 때문에 나는 그곳에 가지 못했다.)

22. *keep ~ in mind = ~를 명심하다*

Keep this proverb **in mind**.

(이 격언을 명심하라.)

23. *lest ~should ~; for fear ~should ~ = ~가 ~하지 않도록*

No holidays were allowed **lest** the habit of work **should** be broken.

(일하는 습관이 깨지는 것을 방지하기 위해 휴가는 허용되지 않았다.)

24. *make A from B = B를 A로 만들다(화학적 변화)*

We **make** butter **from** milk.

(우리는 우유로 버터를 만든다.)

25. make A out of B = B로 A를 만들다(물리적 변화)

Can you **make** pants **out of** that cloth?

(당신은 그 천으로 바지를 만들 수 있습니까?)

26. much [still] more ~ = 훨씬 많이 ~은 말할 것도 없다

He can speak French, **much more** English.

(그는 프랑스어를 할 줄 아는데, 영어는 더욱 잘한다.)

27. neither A nor B = A도 아니고 B도 아닌

My father **neither** drinks **nor** smokes.

(아버지는 술도 담배도 안 하신다.)

28. never ~ but ~ = ~하면 꼭 ~하다(~하지 않으면 ~하지 않는다)

It **never** rains **but** it pours.

(비가 왔다 하면 퍼붓는다.)

29. not ~ any more = 더 이상 ~이 아니다

We don't have to wear school uniforms **any more**.

(우리는 더 이상 교복을 입을 필요가 없다.)

30. not better than ~ = 고작 ~

He is **not better than** a schoolmaster.

(그는 고작 교사일 뿐이다.)

31. not~both ~ = ~ 둘 모두를~하지 않다

I don't know **both** of the sisters.

(나는 그 두 자매 모두를 모른다.)

32. as if [though]=마치 ~한 듯

He speaks as if he knew everything.

(그는 마치 모든 것을 알고 있는 것처럼 말한다.)

33. not A but B = A가 아니라 B이다

He's **not** a fool **but** a genius

(그는 바보가 아니라 천재이다.)

34. not less than ~ = 적어도 ~

This camera did **not** cost **less than** $100.

(이 카메라를 사는 데 적어도 100달러는 들었다.)

35. not only A but (also) B = B as well as A = A뿐만 아니라 B도

She can speak **not only** English **but (also)** French.

(그녀는 영어뿐만 아니라 불어도 잘한다.)

36. not so much A as B = B rather than A~ = A라기 보다는 B이다

He is **not so much** a doctor **as** a scientist.

(= He is a scientist **rather than** a doctor.)

(그는 의사라기보다는 오히려 과학자이다.)

37. not that ~, but that ~ = ~가 아니라 ~이다

Not that he resembles a monkey, **but that** a monkey resembles him.

(그가 원숭이를 닮은 것이 아니라 원숭이가 그를 닮았다.)

38. none the less = 그럼에도 불구하고, 그래도

I love him **none the less** for his faults.

(나는 그의 결점에도 불구하고 그를 사랑한다.)

39. not[never] ~until ~ = ~ 하고 나서야 ~하다

We do **not** know the blessing of health **until** we lose it.

(우리는 건강을 잃고 나서야 비로소 건강의 고마움을 안다.)

40. nothing of ~ = 조금도 ~가 없다[아니다]

I am **nothing of** a scholar.

(나는 학식이 조금도 없다.)

41. on one hand——, on the other hand ~ = ~ 한편으로는~, 다른 한편으로는 ~

On one hand I have to look after the children; **on the other hand** I have a lot of customers to deal with.

(나는 한편으로는 아이들을 돌보아야 하고, 다른 한편으로는 많은 손님들을 상대해야 한다.)

42. one ~, the other ~ = (둘 중) 하나는 ~이고 다른 하나는 ~.이다

He has two brothers. **One** is in Paris, and **the other** in New York.

(그는 두 명의 형이 있다. 한명은 파리에 있고 다른 한 명은 뉴욕에
있다.)

*43. one −, another ~, the third~ = (셋 중) 하나는 −, 또 다른 하나는~,
나머지 하나는 ~이다*

Here are three flowers : **one** is a lily, **another** is a rose and **the
third** is a tulip.

(꽃이 세 송이 있다. 하나는 백합이고, 다른 하나는 장미이고, 나머지
하나는 튤립이다.)

44. one ~, the others = (셋 이상 중) 하나는 ~이고 나머지 모두는 ~이다

One of m sisters is a nurse, and **the others** are teachers.

(나의 누나들 중 한명은 간호사이고, 나머지는 모두 교사이다.)

45. owe A to B = A는 B의 덕택이다.

I **owe** my success **to** my mother.

(나의 성공은 어머니 덕택이다.)

46. remind A of B = A에게 B를 생각나게 하다

You **remind** me **of** your mother.

(너는 나에게 너의 어머니를 생각나게 한다.)

47. *rob A of B = A에게서 B를 빼앗다*

The man **robbed** her **of** her watch.

(그 남자는 그녀에게서 시계를 훔쳤다.)

48. *see A off = A를 배웅하다*

Namsu came to **see** me **off**.

(남수가 나를 배웅 나왔다.)

49. *so that A may ~ ; in order that A may[can] ~ =A가~할 수 있도록*

He works hard so **that** his family **may** live in comfort.

(그는 가족들이 편안하게 살 수 있도록 열심히 일한다.)

50. *some ~, others ~ =어떤 사람은 ~하고, 어떤 사람은 ~하다*

Some love wrestling; **others** do not.

(레슬링을 좋아하는 사람도 있고 싫어하는 사람도 있다.)

51. *such ~ that ~ = ~해서 ~하다*

He is **such** an honest man **that** everybody trusts him.

(그는 매우 정직한 사람이기 때문에 사람들은 그를 신뢰한다.)

52. *take A by the hand ~ = A의 손을 잡다*

Grandmother **took** me **by the hand**.

(할머니는 내 손을 잡았다.)

53. thank A for ~ = ~에 대해 A에게 감사하다

Thank you **for** you kind help.

(친절히 도와주서서 감사합니다.)

54. the + 비교급~, the + 비교급 ~ =~할수록 더욱~하다

The *more* you have, **the** *more* you want.

(가지면 가질수록 더 갖고 싶어진다.)

The *older* we grow, the *weaker* becomes our eyesight.

(나이를 먹으면 먹을수록 우리의 시력은 약해진다.)

55. the last person to ~ =결코 ~할 사람이 아니다

He was **the last person to** commit suicide.

(그는 결코 자살할 사람이 아니다.)

56. the one[former]~, the other[latter] ~ =전자는~이고 후자는 ~이다

I have a Thunderbird and a Lincoln; **the one**[former] is white and **the other**[latter] is black.

(나는 선더버드와 링컨을 갖고 있는데, 전자(선더버드)는 흰 색이고 후자(링컨)은 검은색이다.)

57. the very + 명사 = 바로 그~

This is **the very** *book* I have long been looking for.
(이것은 내가 오랫동안 찾아온 바로 그 책이다.)

His **very** *son* could not understand him.
(그의 친자식조차 그를 이해하지 못했다.)

58. too~to ~ = 너무 ~해서 ~하지 못하다

We arrived **too** late **to** catch the last train.
(=We arrived so late that we couldn't catch the last train.)
(우리는 너무 늦어서 마지막 기차를 타지 못했다.)

59. would rather [sooner] ~.than ~ = ~ 하느니 차라리 ~하다

I **would rather** *die* **than** *marry* her.
(그녀와 결혼하느니 차라리 죽겠다.)

60. A is no more B than C is B. = A가 B가 아닌 것은 C가 B가 아닌 것과 같다

A whale **is no more** a fish **than** a horse **is**.
(고래가 물고기가 아닌 것은 말이 물고기가 아닌 것과 같다.)

Economic laws *can* **no more** be evaded **than** *can* gravitation
(경제 법칙을 피할 수 없는 것은 중력을 피할 수 없는 것과 같다)

1. S + V + ★ + ★ + ★
    ①   ⑤   ④   ③   ②

He arrived in Seoul by bus yesterday

2. S + ★ + ★ + V + ★+ ★
    ③   ②   ①   ⑥   ⑤   ④

Eyeglasses with a camera and speaker in them may whisper
into your ears directly.

3. ★ + ★ + S + V + ★ + ★
    ②   ①   ③   ⑥   ⑤   ④

At the touch of a button, you will talk to people across the ocean.

4. S + V + 명사 + to부정사 + ★ + ★

                        O   OC

   ① ⑥ ②   ⑤   ④ ③

  (~은,는,이,가)   (~하도록,~을,를)

I want you to receive Jesus as your Lord right now.

5. S + V + 명사 + 원형부정사 + ★ + ★

   ① ⑥ ②   ⑤   ④ ③

  (~은,는,이,가)   (~하도록,~을,를)

He looked at her sleep alone in the room.

6. S + V + 명사 + 분사 + ★ + ★

   ① ⑥ ② ⑤ ④ ③

       (~은,는,이,가) (~하도록,~을,를)

I saw a man searching for something in the park.

7. S + V + 명사 + 명사 + ★ + ★

   ① ⑥ ② ⑤ ④ ③

     (~을,~를) (~로)

He called the dog Big Bill for some reasons.

8. S + V̲ + 명사 + 명사 + ★

  수여동사(~에게)(~을,를)

   ① ⑤ ② ④ ③

They gave him lots of money for his hospitality.

9. S + V + that(which, how, where) + S + V + ★

① ⑤ ② ④ ③

Nobody would believe that I was innocent.

I don't know where the noise is coming from.

10. S + V + 명사 + that + S + V + ★

① ⑥ ⑤ ② ④ ③

He is reading the book that she has lent him.

11. S + V + 명사 + that + V + ★ + ★

① ⑥ ⑤ ④ ③ ②

He is a vegetarian that doesn't eats meat or fish.

12. When (if, where, ⋯) + S + V + ★ + ★, S + V + ★ + ★

⑤ ① ④ ③ ② ⑥ ⑨ ⑧ ⑦

When he was out on a trip, his father died unexpectedly in the car accident.

13. S + V + ★ + and + V + ★ + ★

① ③ ② ④ ⑦ ⑥ ⑤

It was born in the zoo and has lived there for a long time.

14. S + V + ★ + and + ★ + ★

① ⑥ ② ③ ⑤ ④

I love my family and friends in class.

15. S + V + ★ + ★ + and + V + ★ + ★

　　① 　④ 　③ 　② 　　⑤ 　⑧ 　⑦ 　⑥

She opened the card on the de나 and found these words printed

on it.

16. S + V + ★ + ★, ~ing + ★ + ★

　　① 　④ 　③ 　② 　　⑦ 　　⑥ 　⑤

He left the room quietly, following the man in secret.

17. S + V + ★, ~ing + ★ .

　　③ 　⑤ 　④ 　　② 　　①

The audience gave her a big hand, cheering loudly.

18. <u>There is(are)</u> + 명사 + ★ + ★

　　　　　④ 　　　　③ 　② 　①

　　　(있다)　S(은,는,이,가)

There was a king named Alexander.

19. <u>There is(are)</u> + 명사 + + who + V + ★ + ★ + ★

　　　　　⑥ 　　　　⑤ 　　　　　④ 　③ 　② 　①

There were few women who had such jobs like taxi drivers and

fire fighters.

20. 동명사 + ★ + ★ + V + ★ + ★

　　　③ 　　② 　① 　⑥ 　⑤ 　④

　(~하는 것은)

Asking him a question is a waste of time.

21. To부정사 + ★ + ★ + V + ★ + ★
       ③   ② ① ⑥ ⑤ ④

(〜하는 것은)

To be always on time is the duty of a gentleman.

22. S + <u>be동사</u> + <u>to부정사</u> + ★ + ★
  ①   ⑤   ④   ③ ②

    (〜이다)   (〜 것)

My dream is to become president of Korea

23. S + <u>be동사</u> + <u>동명사</u> + ★ + ★
  ①   ⑤   ④   ③ ②

    (〜이다)   (〜것)

My hobby is collecting coins of other countries.

24. S + V (동명사를 목적어로 취하는 동사) + 동명사 + ★ + ★
  ① ⑤   ④   ③ ②

                           (〜을, 를,〜하도록)

You shouldn't postpone answering her letter any longer.

25. To부정사 + ★,   S + V + ★ + ★
    ②   ① ③ ⑥ ⑤ ④

(〜하기 위해)

To study English, he went to America at the age of 12.

26. S + V + To부정사 + ★ + ★

   ① ⑤   ④   ③ ②

      (～하기 위해)

He is studying to find the solution to the problem.

27. S + V(to 부정사를 목적어로 취하는 동사) + To부정사 + ★ + ★

   ① ⑤   ④   ③ ②

                  (～을,를,하도록)

We are planning to visit Africa this winter.

28. S + V(sad, happy, sorry, rejoice, bad) + To부정사 + ★

   ① ④   ③   ②

                  (～하니)

She was very sad to see him in prison.

29. S + V + 형용사 + To부정사 + ★ + ★

   ① ⑥ ⑤   ④   ③ ②

      (～하기에)

The Bible is strong enough to save our soul from depravity.

30. S + V(awake, grow up) + To부정사 + ★ + ★

   ① ②   ⑤   ④ ③

He grew up to become a famous movie star in America.

UNIT 11 종합 연습 문제

다음의 영어 문장에서 주어, 동사, 목적어, 보어, 구, 절에 선을 긋고
해석공식에 맞추어 해석해 보시요.

1. The spacious room has much furniture.

2. Much clothing is needed in cold countries.

3. To tell him directly will make him angry.

4. She was a mother of three children.

5. To use a bag only once is a waste.

6. Water is composed of oxygen and hydrogen.

7. Asking him the question will be a waste of time.

8. To be always on time is the duty of a gentleman.

9. The water in this glass is not good to drink.

10. The milk in the bottle went bad.

11. The beauty of the scenery is beyond description.

12. To eat too much is bad for the health.

♣단어학습♣

always	부) 늘, 언제나, 항상	angry	형) 노한, 성난
ask	동) ~을 묻다. 부탁하다		
bad	형) 나쁜, 불량한 go bad –(음식 등이)상하다		
bag	명) 가방	beauty	명) 아름다움, 미
beyond	전) ~의 저쪽에, 너머에, ~보다나은	bottle	명) 병
child	명) 어린이 복수 – children	clothing	명) 의복, 의류
cold	형) 추운, 찬		
compose	동) ~을 구성하다, ~의 일부를 이루다 (be composed of~; ~으로 이루어지다)		
country	명) 나라, 지방 복수–countries	description	명) 서술, 기술, 해설
directly	부) 직접적으로, 똑바로, 바로	drink	동) 마시다
duty	명) 의무, 책임, 도의	eat	동) 먹다
furniture	명) 가구	gentleman	명) 신사
glass	명) 유리	good	형) 좋은, 훌륭한
health	명) 건강	him	(he의 목적격) 그를, 그에게
hydrogen	명) 수소(원소 중 제일 가벼운 기체)	make	동) 만들다, 야기하다, 시키다, 되다
mother	명) 어머니, 모친	much	형) (양이) 많은
need	동) ~을 필요로 하다	once	부) 한번, 일찍이, 한때

only	부) 오직, 단지	oxygen	명) 산소
question	명) 질문	room	명) 방, 실(室)
scenery	명) 풍경, 경관, 경치	spacious	형) 넓은, 거대한, (도량이)넓은
tell	동) ~을 말하다, 알리다	time	명) 시간, 때, 세월 on time – 정각에
too	부) 매우, 또한, 게다가	use	동) ~를 사용하다, 이용하다
waste	명) 낭비, 동)~을 낭비하다, 허비하다	water	명) 물
will	(미래시제조동사)~일 것이다		

13. ^{1}In the beginning God created the heavens and the earth. ^{2}The earth was empty, a formless mass cloaked in darkness. And the Spirit of God was hovering over its surface. (Genesis 1:1~2)

14. ^{1}So the creation of the heavens and the earth and everything in them was completed. ^{2}On the seventh day, having finished his task, God rested from all his work. ^{3}And God blessed the seventh day and declared it holy, because it was the day when he rested from his work of creation. ^{4}This is the account of the creation of the heavens and the earth. When the LORD God made the heavens and the earth, ^{5}there were no plants or grain growing on the earth, for the LORD God had not sent any rain. And no one was there to cultivate the soil. ^{6}But water came up out of the ground and watered all the land. ^{7}And the LORD God formed a man's body from the dust of the ground and breathed into it the breath of life. And the man became a living person. ^{8}Then the LORD God planted a garden in Eden, in the east, and there he placed the man he had created. ^{9}And the LORD

God planted all sorts of trees in the garden—beautiful trees that produced delicious fruit. At the center of the garden he placed the tree of life and the tree of the knowledge of good and evil. [10]A river flowed from the land of Eden, watering the garden and then dividing into four branches. [11]One of these branches is the Pishon, which flows around the entire land of Havilah, where gold is found. (Genesis 2:1~11)

15. [1]In the beginning the Word already existed. He was with God, and he was God. [2]He was in the beginning with God. [3]He created everything there is. Nothing exists that he didn't make. [4]Life itself was in him, and this life gives light to everyone. [5]The light shines through the darkness, and the darkness can never extinguish it. [6]God sent John the Baptist [7]to tell everyone about the light so that everyone might believe because of his testimony. [8]John himself was not the light; he was only a witness to the light. [9]The one who is the true light, who gives light to everyone, was going to come into the world. (John 1:1~9)

♠단어학습♠

account	명) 설명, 보고	all	형) 전부의, 내내의, 모든
already	부) 이미, 벌써	any	형) 무슨, 조금도
baptist	명) 침례(세례)주는 사람	beautiful	형)아름다운
become	동) ~이 되다, 일어나다		
beginning	명) 시초, 최초 in the beginning-태초에		
believe	동) 믿다	body	명) 몸, 육체
branch	명) 가지, 부문		

breathe	동) 숨쉬다, ~into:~에게 새 생명을 불어넣다		
center	명) 중심, 중앙	cloak	동) (~ in) ~으로 덮다, ~을 은폐하다
come up	동) 떠오르다	complete	형) 완성된, 철저한, 동) ~을 완성하다
create	동) ~을 창조하다, ~을 만들어 내다	cultivate	동) ~을 갈다, 경작하다, 재배하다
darkness	명) 어둠	delicious	형) 맛있는
divide	동) 나누다 ~into ☆ ~을 ☆로 나누다		
dust	명) 먼지	earth	명) (the ~) -땅, 지상, 대지, 육지
east	명) 동쪽	empty	형) 빈, 아무도 없는
entire	형) 전체의, 완전한	everyone	대) 누구든지, 모두
everything	대) 모든 것	evil	명) 악, 악의 형) 나쁜, 악질의
exist	동) 존재하다, 실재하다	extinguish	동) (불을)끄다, 소멸시키다
finish	동) ~을 끝내다, 종결하다	flow	동) 흐르다, 순환하다
form	동) 형성하다	formless	형) 모양이 없는, 실체가 없는
fruit	명) 과일	garden	명) 정원
give	동) ~을 주다	God	명) 신, 하나님, 창조주
gold	명) 금	good	명) 좋은 것, 선 형)좋은, 충분한
grain	명) 곡식알, 낱알	ground	명) 땅
grow	동) 자라다, 발육하다	heaven	명) 하늘, 천국 (보통 the heavens)
hover	동) 공중을 날다, 빙빙 맴돌다 (~over)	itself	대) 그 자신, 바로그것
knowledge	명) 지식, 학문	land	명) 뭍, 육지
life	명) 생명, 삶	mass	명) 덩어리
no	아니오	nothing	대) 아무것도 ~아니다 명)무
place	명) 장소, 동) ˜을 놓다, 배치하다	plant	명) 식물 동)~ (씨)를 뿌리다
produce	동) ~을 제조하다, 생산하다	rain	명) 비, 동) 비가 내리다
rest	동) 쉬다, 명) 휴식	river	명) 강,하천
send	동) 보내다	shine	동) 빛나다, 밝게 빛나다
soil	명) 흙, 토양	sort	명) 종류, 품종
spirit	명) 정신, 영혼	surface	명) 표면, 외면, 외관
task	명) 일, 직무	testimony	명) 증언, 증거, 증명
them	대) ((they의 목적격)) 그들을, 그것들을		
there	부) 거기에, (be동사와 함께 존재) 있다		
through	전) ~을 통과하여,~을 통하여	true	형) 참된, 진실의
water	명) 물	witness	명) 목격자, 증인
word	명) 말, 언어		
work	명) 일, 노동, 공부 동) 일하다, 작업하다		

Amazing Predictions for the Future

Everyone wonders what the future will bring. In your great-grandchildren's lifetime, dinner might be served by robots, and airplanes might fly without pilots. Who knows? Maybe we won't even need airplanes to fly from place to place.

Our vision of the future keeps changing. At your age, your great-grandparents never dreamed that personal computers would receive e-mail letters from anywhere in the world. In the same way, tomorrow's wonders are probably beyond our imagination. Even so, it's fun to try to guess what the future will bring.

COMPUTER-WEAR

In the future, messages from a portable computer may appear on an eyeglass lens. Also, eyeglasses with a camera and speaker in them may whisper into your ear the name of the person you're facing — in case you've forgotten it. Even clothes will be smart. High-tech clothes will warm or cool you any time you want.

VIDEO WRISTWATCHES

In the future, you'll be able to phone home with video wristwatches. At the touch of a button, you'll talk to people across the street or even across the ocean. Smile! A video image of your face will be sent along with your voice.

VIRTUAL REALITY

Suppose you are stuck in the house. Don't be sad. You'll slip on a virtual reality (VR) helmet and enjoy a virtual party with your friends on a computer. You might use a VR helmet to play along inside a television game show, join your favorite rock band onstage, or leap into an action film. The future will be bright for couch potatoes!

DOOR-TO-DOOR DRIVERLESS TAXIS

No cars in the future? No problem! At a taxi station, you'll simply say your destination into a voice-recognition machine. A door will open to a small, automated taxi as the fare is electronically paid from your bank account. Then the taxi will take you to your destination.

MIRACLE CHIPS

"Billy? Where are you?" When a child gets lost, the parents will find him or her without difficulty, Every child will carry a microchip, and it will help the parents to find them. The same kind of chip could also serve as a library card, driver's license, and medical record.

Wonders in the future are probably beyond our imagination. "We study the future so we can prepare for tomorrow," explains Joseph Coates, a futurist from Washington, D.C. Futurists help companies and governments plan ahead – but not too far ahead. Technology is changing quickly, so predictions that look beyond the next 30 years would be mostly guesswork. "Looking into the future is an art, not a science," says Coates.

♣단어학습♣

account	명) 계좌	across	전) ~을 가로질러, 횡단하여
ahead	부) 앞쪽에, 앞으로	airplane	명) 비행기
amazing	형) 놀랄만한	anywhere	부) 어디든지 명) 어딘가
appear	동) 나타나다	art	명) 예술
automate	동) ~을 자동화하다	bring	동) ~을 가져오다, 초래하다
carry	동) ~을 운반하다	chairman	명) 의장, 사회자, 회장
chip	명) 칩, 반도체 소자	company	명) 친구, 동료, 회사
deal	동) 대처하다, 처리하다, 논하다 (~with)	destination	명) 목적지, 행선지
difficulty	명) 어려움, 곤란	dream	명) 꿈, 동) 꿈을 꾸다
driver	명) 운전자	electronically	형) 전자의, 온라인의
explain	동) 설명하다	eyeglass	명) 외알안경, 접안렌즈
face	동) 마주대하다, 직면하다 명) 얼굴	fare	명) 요금, 운임
fly	동) 날다	forget	동) 잊다 과거-forgot
futurist	명) 미래신자, 인류 진보의 신봉자	government	명) 정부
grandchild	명) 손자, 손녀 복) grandchildren	guess	동) 추측하다
guesswork	명) 어림짐작	high-tech	명) 첨단기술
imagination	명) 상상	issue	명) 공포, 발행, 쟁점
library	명) 도서관, 문고	license	명) 자격증
lifetime	명) 일생, 생애	lost	형) 잃어버린, lose의 과거형-잃다
medical	형) 의학의, 의술의	message	명) 알림, 통지, 메시지
miracle	명) 기적, 신기	mostly	부) 대부분의, 주로
next	형) 다음의	ocean	명) 대양, 해양, 바다
pay	동) 지불하다	personal	형) 개인의, 사적인, 개인용의
plan	동) 계획하다	portable	형) 휴대용의, 간편한
prediction	명) 예언, 예보	prepare	동) 준비하다
press	동) ~을 누르다, 밀어 붙이다.	probably	부) 아마도

quickly	부) 빨리	receive	동) 받다
record	명) 기록 동) ~을 기록하다	replace	동) ~을 대신하다, 제자리에 놓다
ruling	명) 지배, 통치 형) 지배하는, 유력한	sad	형) 슬픈
serve	동) ~에 봉사하다,(음식 등을) 제공하다	simply	부) 간단히, 간편하게
slip	동) 미끄러지다	smart	형) 영리한, 빈틈없는
strike	동) ~을 가하다, 공격하다	study	동) 공부하다
suppose	동) ~이라 가정하다, 상상하다	technology	명) 기술
vision	명) 시력, 환상, 통찰력, 미래상	warm	형) 따뜻한
whisper	동) 속삭이다, 밀담하다 명) 속삭임	without	부) 없이
wristwatch	명) 손목시계		

♣단어학습♣

science	명)과학	escape	동)달아나다, 탈출하다
ask	동)묻다, 요청하다	yourself	대)당신자신
purpose	명)목적, 용도, 의도	express	동)표현하다
own	형)자기소유의	feeling	명)촉감, 감각
write	동)~을쓰다	fact	명)사실
information	명)정보	persuade	동)설득하다
mind	명)마음	subject	명)주제, 화제
each	형)각자의, 각각의	first	형)최초의, 첫번째의

pack	명)꾸러미, 짐 동)짐을 꾸리다, 싸다	trick	명)책략, 계략, 속임수
wave	명)파도,물결, (손)흔들기, 동)손을흔들다	scratch	동)긁다, 할퀴다
stand	동)서다, 서있다	zookeeper	명)(동물원)사육사
bath	명)목욕	cage	명)새장, 우리
promise	명)약속, 계약 동)약속하다	soccer	명)축구
article	명)기사, 논설	newspaper	명)신문
reward	명)보수, 보상,		

official	명)공무원, 관리	offer	동)~을 제공하다
spider	명)거미, 거미같은것	brown	명)갈색, 밤색
weigh	동)저울에 달다. ~을 평가하다	ounce	명)온스 (무게의 단위)
director	명)지도자, 지휘자	capture	동)~을 붙잡다, 체포하다
special	형)특별한	handler	명)다루는 사람
available	형)쓸모있는, 유용한	councilman	명)(지방의회의)의원, 평의원

remind	동)~을 상기시키다	guard	동)지키다, 보호하다
patrol	동)순회하다, 순찰하다	protection	명)보호
second	형)두번째의	urge	동)재촉하다, 주장하다
vote	명)투표, ~을 투표로 결정하다	provide	동)제공하다

Bomba Escapes from the Zoo

When you are writing, ask yourself what your purpose is. Are you writing simply to express your own feelings? Are you writing to give facts and other kinds of information? Are you writing to persuade other people to change their minds about something? The writings that follow are about the same subject. But each has a different purpose. As you read, think about how differently the subject is presented for each purpose.

[1]

I will never forget the first time I saw Bomba the monkey at the Evanstown Zoo. It was a sunny Sunday afternoon. The place was packed with people watching the new monkey. I felt Bomba was doing all of his tricks just for me. If I waved at him, he waved at me. If I scratched my head, he scratched his head. An old man standing by me said, "Well, this monkey sure likes you!"

I never did go to see the zookeepers giving the baby elephant a bath. Instead, I stayed by the monkey cage for two or three hours. I felt sad to leave Bomba, and he seemed sorry to see me go. I promised him I'd be back soon.

Then I got busy with school work, soccer, and all kinds of other things. I was planning to go to see Bomba again this weekend. But now an article in the newspaper says Bomba escaped yesterday. There's a big reward for giving information about

Bomba. I don't want any money. I just want Bomba to be back safely in his cage.

[2]
MONKEY ESCAPES FROM ZOO

A monkey escaped from the Evanstown Zoo yesterday. Zoo officials are offering a $1,000 reward for information.

The spider monkey, known as Bomba, is brown and weighs ten pounds nine ounces. It was born in the zoo and has always lived there.

Andrea Coleman, Director of the Zoo, asks the public not to try to capture the monkey. For the safety of the public and the monkey, special animal handlers will be available 24 hours a day. Anyone having any information about the missing monkey is asked to call Ms. Coleman at the special Missing Animals Hot Line,555-ZOOS.

[3]

Dear Town Councilman Smith:

The escape of Bomba the monkey from the Evanstown Zoo reminds us that we need more guards at the zoo. Because of outs in funding, the number of zoo guards has been cut in half. Instead of two guards patrolling the zoo grounds, there is now only one. There are two reasons to keep two guards on duty at all times. The first reason is for the safety and protection of the animals in the zoo. The second reason is for the safety and protection of the public. I urge you to vote "yes" on the bill that will provide more funding for the zoo.

Growing as a person may take you to new places and present new challenges. These may be stressful, but feeling stress is a natural, necessary part of recognizing a weakness and trying out a new behavior. It is often comfortable and easy to stay the way we are. Giving up old comforts and habits is very hard. It is small wonder that people dislike changing. (수능기출문제)

Since the mid-1990s, teaching Korean to foreigners has made

quiet and steady progress. Many universities now offer Korean language programs in Korea and abroad, and many textbooks have been produced for learners of Korean. Only a small number of foreigners, however, have benefited from this progress. Most foreign workers are being taught by Korean co-workers or volunteers who have no or little teaching experience. Thus, it is necessary to establish better educational programs for teaching the Korean language to foreign workers. (수능기출문제)

♣단어학습♣

by no means	결코 ~ 않은	well off	부유한
rush	동)돌진하다, 갑자기 달려들다 형)바쁜	last	형)최후의, 마지막의
attempt	동)시도하다, 꾀하다 명)시도	catch up	따라잡다
identical	형)똑같은, 동일한	greeting	명)인사, 절
snap	동)찰깍하고 소리나다 (~up)을잡아채다	sign	명)표, 기호
post	동)우송하다sigh명)한숨 동)한숨쉬다,탄식하다		
relief	명)제거, 경감	gift	명)선물

There was a kind woman who made a last attempt to catch up. Seeing a box of 50 identical greeting cards in a shop, she snapped it up, carried it home, and signed 49 cards before midnight. She posted them the next morning and gave a sigh of relief. Then she opened one remaining card, and found these words printed on it : This little card is just to say a gift from me is on the way.(수능기출문제)

♣단어학습♣

supervise	동)감독하다	warehouse	명)창고
offer	동)제공하다	operation	명)작업, 조작
base on	~에 기초를 두다	frequent	형) 자주 일어나는, 빈번한

responsibility   명)책임감   record   명)기록, 동) 기록하다
prove   동)증명하다

Thomas Jefferson once said that what matters is the courage of one's convictions. Do you have the courage which comes from the sincere conviction that you are a person of sound character, an honest, dependable, kind, and caring person ? If you do, you will never have to worry about what others think of you. If you know in your heart that you are a good and decent Person, you can life's challenges head-on and without fear of what others think. (수능기출문제)

♣단어학습♣

approach   접근하다   intersection   교차로 즉시 의식 방향
wheelchair   휠체어   costly lesson   값비싼 교훈

A terrible accident changed my life. A friend and I were driving home from a midnight movie. As we approached an intersection, we stopped at a red light. No cars seemed to be coming, so I decided to go through the red light. Immediately after we started, I lost consciousness. Later I learned that we had hit a car coming from the other direction. That accident made my friend spend the rest of his life in a wheelchair, and I learned a costly lesson. (수능기출문제)

-고급 문장-

1. As the tadpole grows older the cells composing its tail are attacked and absorbed by certain body cells until the tail shrinks and finally disappears completely. [사법고시]

♣단어학습♣
· tadpole : 올챙이   · cell : 세포
· absorb : 흡수하다   · shrink : 줄어들다   · resume : 되찾다.

2. During the American Revolution the people of Canada remained loyal to England although the rebelling colonies tried to persuade them to join the war for independence.
[한국전력]

♣단어학습♣
·revolution : 혁명   · loyal : 충성의
·rebel : 항거하다   ·colony : 거류민
·persuade : 설득하다   ·surrender : 항복하다

3. The Korean economic system does not exist in isolation but is a part of the world-wide economic system. Thus, the economic life of the Korean people is greatly affected by the economic life of all the peoples. [사법고시]

♣단어학습♣
· exist : 존재하다   · isolation : 고립
·affect : 영향을 끼치다   · product : 농산물
· stock market : 증권시장

4. Today, our enormous investment in science and research is the evidence of our faith that science can not only make man richer but it can make man better. [포항공대 대학원]

♣단어학습♣
· enormous : 막대한   · investment : 투자
· research : 연구   · evidence : 증거

5. But in 1799 an officer in Napoleon's army discovered near the Egyptian village of Rosetta a smooth, thick black stone covered with carvings that were divided into three separate sections. [TOEFL]

♣단어학습♣
· officer : 장교   · carvings : 조각
· separate : 분리된   · section : 부분

6. In northern countries many insects and worms that cannot live in winter die when cold weather comes. They leave larvae, or egg, to revive their species the following spring. [행정고시]

♣단어학습♣
· worm : 벌레   · larvae : 유충
· revive : 소생시키다   · species : 종, 종류

7. The animal's mouth is disproportionately large in comparison with his narrow throat. When he fills his mouth with food, he must chew for a long time before he can

swallow. [한국외대 대학원, 행정고시]

♣단어학습♣
· disproportionately : 어울리지 않게
· in comparison with : ~와 비교해서
· throat ; 목구멍 · gnaw : 갉아먹다
· swallow : 삼키다

8. If democracy is to survive ,above all the thing that a teacher should endeavor to produce in his pupils is the kind of tolerance that springs from an endeavor to understand those who are different from ourselves. [한양대 대학원]

♣단어학습♣
· democracy : 민주주의   · survive : 살아남다
· above all : 특히, 우선   · endeavor : 노력, 노력하다
· tolerance : 아량, 관용   · spring from : ~에서 생기다

9. Just when many of the nation's contractors were looking into moving out of the industry, the unfortunate result of the earthquake has created an enormous demand for construction. [TOEIC]

♣단어학습♣
· enormous : 엄청난   · contractor : 토건업자, 도급업자
· look into : 조사하다   · demand : 수요

10. Drama thrived in India a long time ago, and since the plays presented there always had happy endings, Hindu theatergoers were strangers to tragedies. [외무고시]

♣단어학습♣

· thrive : 번창하다   · theatergoer : 관객

· tragedy : 비극   · costume : 의복

부록1 : OMS공식집

부록2 : 연습문제 해설

ONE - STOP ENGLISH

〈약어표〉

S(주어), V(동사), O(목적어), C(보어), O'(의미상의 목적어), C'(의미상의 보어),

a(형용사), a.p=phrase(형용사구), a.c=clause (형용사절)

ad(부사), ad.p(부사구), ad.c(부사절), conj=conjunction (접속사)

주어(S) 공식 6가지

1. 명사 : 고유, 보통, 집합, 물질, 추상명사

2. 대명사 : 인칭, 소유, 지시, 부정, 의문대명사

* 전치사+명사, 대명사는 주어가 될 수 없다.

3. To 부정사(to+동사원형)

To 부정사 + ★ +★ + V +★

4. 동명사(동사원형+ing)

동명사 + ★ +★ + V +★

5. 절(S+V를 포함하는 하나의 문장) 주어

절단어 + S + V1+ ★+ V2 + ★

6. 비인칭주어 (It is + 시간, 날씨, 날자. 요일, 명암, 거리 등)

동사(V) 공식 8가지

1. be동사 (am, are, is, was, were)

2. 일반동사

3. 조동사+동사원형

4. 숙어동사 (전치사로 끝, '~을~다'로 해석)

5. 12능동, 8수동

6. 조동사 완료

7. be to 동사 – 의무, 예정, 운명, 가능, 의도

8. 관용어구 동사

목적어(O) 공식 7가지

O1) 일반동사 + 명사(대) ☞ 명사 앞에 전치사가 오면 안 된다.

O2) 숙어동사 + 명사(대) 이 때 명사 앞의 전치사는 숙어동사의 마지막 자리이다.

O3) 동사+ to 부정사

O4) 동사+ 동명사

O5) 동사+〔to 부정사 or 동명사〕

O6) 동사+ 절〔(that, what, where, how…) + S + V + ☆〕

O7) 수여동사 + 명사 + 명사(절) (~에게 ~을)

목적어+보어(O+C) 공식 5가지

O+C1) 동사+ 명사 + 명사

O+C2) 동사+ 명사 + 형용사

O+C3) 동사+ 명사 + To부정사

O+C4) 지각동사, 사역동사 + 명사 + 동사원형(원형부정사)

O+C5) 지각동사(일반적으로) + 명사 + 분사(과거 및 현재분사)

보어(C) 공식 6가지

C1) be, become + 명사, 대명사

C2) 동사+ 형용사

C3) 동사+ 분사

C4) be동사+ to부정사

C5) be동사+ 동명사

C6) be동사+〔that + S + V + ☆〕절보어

형용사구(a.p) 공식 3가지

1) 전명구(전치사 +명사)

2) 부정사구(to +동사원형)

3) 분사구(현재분사~ing /과거분사 ~ed)

형용사절(a.c) 공식 2가지

1) 관계대명사: Who, whose, whom, which, that

2) 관계부사: When, where, why, how, that

부사구(ad.p) 공식 3가지

1) 전명구(전치사 +명사)

2) 부정사구(to +동사원형)

3) 분사구(현재분사~ing /과거분사 ~ed)

부사절(ad.c) 공식 9가지

1) 시간 부사절

2) 장소 부사절

3) 원인 · 이유 부사절

4) 조건 부사절

5) 양보 부사절

6) 목적 부사절

7) 결과 부사절

8) 양태, 비율 부사

9) 비교 부사절

1. The spacious room has much furniture.

	S		V		O1
	1		3		2

그 넓은 방은 많은 가구를 가지고 있다. (그 넓은 방에는 많은 가구가 있다.)

2. Much clothing is needed in cold countries.

	S		V		ad,p
	1		3		2

많은 의류가 추운 나라에서 필요하다

3. To tell him directly will make him angry.

S	O1'	ad	V	O	C2
3	2	1	6	4	5

직접 그에게 말하는 것은 그를 화나게 만들 것이다.

4. She was a mother of three children.

S	V	C1		a,p
1	4	3		2

그 여자는 세 아이의 엄마였다.

5. To use a bag only once is a waste.

S	O1'		ad	V	C1
3	2		1	5	4

단 한 번 가방을 사용한다는 것은 낭비이다.

6. Water is composed of oxygen and hydrogen.

	S		V		ad,p
	1		3		2

물은 산소와 수소로 이루어져 있다.

7. Asking him the question will be a waste of time.

S	O7	O7	V	C1	a.p
3	1	2	6	5	4

그에게 질문을 한다는 것은 시간 낭비일 것이다.

8. To be always on time is the duty of a gentleman.

S	ad	ad.p	V	C1	a.p
3	2	1	6	5	4

제 시간에 항상 있다는 것은(온다는 것은) 신사의 의무이다.

9. The water in this glass is not good to drink.

S	a.p	V	C2	ad.p
2	1	5	4	3

이 잔 속의 물은 마시기에 좋지 않다.

10. The milk in the bottle went bad.

S	a.p	V	C2
2	1	4	3

그 병의 우유는 상했다.

11. The beauty of the scenery is beyond description.

S	a.p	V	ad.p
2	1	4	3

그 광경의 아름다움은 표현 할 수가 없다.

12. To eat too much is bad for the health.

S	ad	V	C2	ad.p
2	1	5	4	3

너무 많이 먹는 것은 건강에 나쁘다.

13. In the beginning God created the heavens and the earth. The earth was empty,

ad,p	S	V	O1	S	V	C2
1	2	4	3	1	3	2

a formless mass (was)cloaked in darkness. And the Spirit of God was hovering over its surface.

S	V	ad,p	conj	S	a,p	V	ad,p
1	3	2	1	3	2	5	4

처음에(태초에) 하나님께서 하늘과 땅을 만드셨다. 땅은 비었고, 형체 없는 덩어리는 어둠으로 덮혔다. 그리고 하나님의 영은 그것의(땅의) 표면 위에 선회하고 계셨다.(운행하고 계셨다)(Genesis 1:1~2)

14. [1]So the creation of the heavens and the earth and everything in them was completed.

ad	s	a,p	a,p	V	
1	4	2	3	5	

그래서 하늘들과 땅 그리고 그것들(하늘들과 땅) 안에 있는 모든 것의 창조가 완성되었다.

[2]On the seventh day, having finished his task, God rested from all his work.

ad,p	ad,p	O1'	S	V	ad,p
1	3	2	4	6	5

일곱째 날에 그의 일을 마친 하나님께서는 그의 모든 일로부터 쉬셨다.

[3]And God blessed the seventh day and declared it holy, because it was the day (when he rested

conj	S	V	O1	conj	V	O	C3	conj	S	V	C1	a,p	S	V
1	2	4	3	5	8	6	7	9	10	16	15	11	14

from his work of creation.)

ad,p	a,p
13	12

그리고 하나님께서 일곱 째 날을 축복하시고 그것이 거룩하다고 선언하셨다. 왜냐하면 그것은 그가 창조하는 그의 일로부터 쉬셨던 날이었기 때문이다.

[4]This is the account of the creation of the heavens and the earth.

S	V	C1	a,p	a,p
1	5	4	3	2

이것은 하늘들과 땅의 창조에 대한 설명이다.

When the LORD God made the heavens and the earth, [5]there were no plants or grain growing

ad.c	S	V	O1	V	S	ad.p
4	1	3	2	8	7	6

on the earth, for the LORD God had not sent any rain.

ad.p	conj	S	V	O1
5	12	9	11	10

주 하나님이 하늘과 땅을 만드셨을 때 땅 위에 자라나는 아무 식물들과 곡물이 없었다.

왜냐하면 주 하나님께서 어떠한 비도 내리지 않게 하셨기 때문이다.

And no one was there to cultivate the soil.

conj	S	V	a.p	O1'
1	2	5	4	3

그리고 땅을 경작할 아무 사람도 없었다.

[6]But water came up out of the ground and watered all the land. And the LORD God formed a

conj	S	V	ad.p	conj	V	O1	conj	S	V
1	2	4	3	5	7	6	1	2	6

man's body from the dust of the ground and breathed into it the breath of life.

O1	ad.p	a.p	conj	V	ad.p	O1	a.p
5	4	3	7	11	10	9	8

그러나 물이 땅 밖으로 솟아나왔고 모든 땅을 적셨다. 그리고 주 하나님께서 땅의 흙(먼지)으로부터 인간의 몸을 만드셨고, 생기를 그것(사람의 몸) 안으로 불어 넣었다.

[7]And the man became a living person.

conj	S	V	C1
1	2	4	3

그리고 그 남자는 살아 있는 사람이 되었다.

[8]Then the LORD God planted a garden in Eden, in the east, and there he placed the man (that)

ad	S	V	O1	ad.p	ad.p	conj	ad	S	V	O1	a.c
1	2	6	5	4	3	7	8	9	13	12	

he had created.

S	V
10	11

그때에 주 하나님께서 동쪽의 에덴에 동산을 조성하셨고 거기에 하나님께서 그가 만든 사람을 두셨다.

[9]And the LORD God planted all sorts of trees in the garden—beautiful trees that

Conj	S	V	O1	ad.p	동격(all sorts of trees)	a.c
1	2	5	4	3	8	

produced delicious fruit.

V	O1
7	6

그리고 주 하나님께서는 동산 안에 모든 종류의 나무들을 심으셨다 ?(그 나무들은) 맛있는 과일을 생산해 내는 아름다운 나무들(이었다.)

At the center of the garden,

ad.p	a.p
2	1

he placed the tree of life and the tree of the knowledge of good and evil.

S	V	O1	a.p	conj	O1	a.p	a.p
3	10	5	4	6	9	8	7

그 동산의 중앙에 그는 생명의 나무와 선과 악에 관한 지식의 나무를 두셨다.

[10]A river flowed from the land of Eden, watering the garden and then dividing into four

S	V	ad.p	a.p	ad.p	O1′	conj	ad	ad.p	ad.p
1	4	3	2	6	5	7	8	10	9

branches.

한 강이 에덴의 땅으로부터 흘렀다. 그리고 그 동산을 적셨고 그런 다음 네 지류로 나누어졌다.

¹¹One of these branches is the Pishon, which flows around the entire land of Havilah,

S	a.p		V	C1	a.c	V	ad.p		a.p
2	1		4	3	5	8	7		6

where gold is found.

a.c	S	V
9	10	11

이 지류들 중의 하나가 비손(강)인데, 이 비손(강)은 하윌라의 온 땅을 돌아 흐른다. 그런데 거기서 금이 발견된다.

15. ¹In the beginning, the Word already existed. He was with God. And he was God.

ad.p		S	ad	V	S	V	ad.p		conj	S	V	C1
1		3	2	4	1	3	2		1	2	4	3

처음에 (태초에) 이미 말씀이 존재했다. 그는 하나님과 함께 계셨다. 그는 하나님이셨다.

²He was in the beginning with God. ³He created everything (that) there is,

S	V	ad.p	ad.p	S	V	O1	a.c	V
1	4	3	2	1	4	3		2

그는 하나님과 함께 태초에 계셨다.   그는 있는 모든 것을 창조하셨다.

Nothing exists (that he didn't make). ⁴Life itself was in him, and this life gives light to everyone.

S	V	a.c	S	V	S	V	ad.p		conj	s	V	O1	ad.p
3	4	1	2		1	3	2		4	5	8	7	6

그가 만들지 않은 아무것도 존재하지 않는다. 생명 그 자체가 그 안에 있었고, 이 생명은 모든 사람들에게 빛을 준다.

⁵The light shines through the darkness, and the darkness can never extinguish it.

S	V	ad.p		conj	s		v	o1
1	3	2		4	5		7	6

그 빛이 어둠을 뚫고 비치고, 그 어두움이 그것을 결코 끌 수 없다.

⁶God sent John the Baptist ⁷to tell everyone about the light so that everyone might believe

S	V	O		C3	O1'	ad.p	ad.c	s	v
1	10	6		9	8	7	5	2	4

because of his testimony.

ad.p
3

하나님께서는 모든 사람들이 세례 요한의 그의 증거 때문에 믿게 하기 위하여 그가(세례 요한) 그 빛에 관하여 말하도록 보내셨다.

⁸John himself was not the light; he was only a witness to the light.

s	v	c1	s	v	c1	a.p
1	3	2	1	4	3	2

요한 그 자신은 그 빛이 아니었다. 그는 단지 그 빛에 관한 증인이었다.

⁹The one (who is the true light), (who gives light to everyone), was going to come into the world.

S	a.c	v	c1	a.c	v	o1	ad.p	v	ad.p
7	2	1		3	6	5	4	9	8

참 빛이고, 모든 사람에게 빛을 주는 그 분이 세상 속으로 들어오려 하셨다.(John 1:1~9)

Lesson 1. Amazing Predictions for the Future

Amazing Predictions for the Future

Everyone wonders (what the future will bring).
    S   V   O6   S   V

    1   5   4   2   3

모든 사람들이 미래가 가져다 줄 것이 무엇인가를 궁금해 한다.

In your great-grandchildren's lifetime, dinner might be served by robots, and airplanes might fly
             ad.p   S   V   ad.p   conj   S   V

              1   2   4   3   5   6   8

without pilots.
    ad.p

    7

당신의 증손자 시대에는 저녁 식사가 로버트들에 의해 준비되어지고, 비행기들이 조종사없이 날게 될지도 모른다.

Who knows?
   S   V

   1   2

누가 알겠는가? (아무도 모른다)

Maybe we won't even need airplanes to fly from place to place.
   ad   S   V   O1   ad.p   ad.p

   1   2   6   5   4   3

아마 우리가 이곳 저곳으로 비행하기 위해 심지어 비행기가 필요치 않게 될 것이다.

Our vision of the future keeps changing. At your age, your great-grandparents never dreamed

Our vision	of the future	keeps	changing	At your age,	your great-grandparents	never dreamed
S	a.p	V	C3	ad.p	S	V
2	1	4	3	1	2	8

(that personal computers would receive e-mail letters from anywhere in the world.)

(that	personal computers	would receive	e-mail letters	from anywhere	in the world.)
O6	S	V	O1	a.p	ad.p
	3	7	6	5	4

미래의 우리의 비전은 변화하기를 계속한다.(계속 변화한다) 당신의 시대에 당신의 중조부모님은 개인용 컴퓨터가 전 세계 어떤 곳에서라도 온 이메일 편지를 받게 되리라는 것을 결코 꿈꾸지 않았다.

In the same way, tomorrow's wonders are probably beyond our imagination.

In the same way,	tomorrow's wonders	are	probably	beyond our imagination.
ad.p	S	V	ad	ad.p
1	2	5	3	4

그 같은 식으로 내일의 놀라움은 아마도 우리의 상상너머에 있을 것이다.(미래의 놀라운 일들은 상상을 초월할 것이다.)

Even so, it's fun to try to guess (what the future will bring.)

Even so,	it's	fun	to try	to guess	(what	the future	will bring.)
ad	V C1	S	O5'	O6'	S		V
1	8 7	6	5	3	2		4

비록 그렇긴 해도, 미래가 가져다 줄 것이 무엇인가를 상상해 본다는 것은 재미있다.

COMPUTER-WEAR

컴퓨터웨어

In the future, messages from a portable computer may appear on an eyeglass lens.

In the future,	messages	from a portable computer	may appear	on an eyeglass lens.
ad.p	S	a.p	V	ad.p
1	3	2	5	4

미래에는 휴대용 컴퓨터로부터 온 메시지가 안경의 렌즈에 나타나게 될지 모른다.

Also, eyeglasses with a camera and speaker in them may whisper into your ear the name of the

ad	S	a.p		ad.p	V	ad.p	O1
1	4	3		2	10	9	8

person(that) you're facing — in case you've forgotten it.

a.p	a.c	S	V	ad.c	S	V	O1
7		5	6	4	1	3	2

또한 그 안에 카메라와 스피커가 달린 안경이 당신이 대면하고 있는 사람의 이름을 당신의 귀에다
속삭일지 모른다. 당신이 그것을(이름) 잊어버렸을 경우를 대비해서.

Even clothes will be smart.

ad	s	V	c1
1	2	4	3

심지어 의류까지도 똑똑해질 것이다.

High-tech clothes will warm or cool you any time(that) you want.

S	V	O1	ad.p	a.c	S	V
1	6	5	4		2	3

첨단 의류는 당신이 원하는 어떤 때에라도 당신을 따뜻하게 하거나 시원하게 해 줄 것이다.

VIDEO WRISTWATCHES

비디오 손목시계

In the future, you'll be able to phone home with video wristwatches.

ad.p	S	V	ad	ad.p
1	2	5	4	3

미래에 당신은 비디오 손목시계로 집에 전화를 걸 수 있게 될 것이다.

At the touch of a button, you'll talk to people across the street or even across the ocean

ad.p	a.p	S	V	ad.p	ad.p	conj	ad.p
2	1	3	8	7	4	5	6

버튼을 한 번 누르면 당신은 길 건너 혹은 심지어 바다 건너에 있는 사람들에게 말을 하게 될 것이다.

Smile! A video image of your face will be sent along with your voice.

	S	a.p	V	ad.p
	2	1	4	3

웃으세요. 당신의 얼굴 비디오상이 당신의 목소리와 함께 보내질 것이다.

VIRTUAL REALITY

가상현실

Suppose(that) you are stuck in the house. Don't be sad.

V	o6	S	V	ad.p	V	C2
4		1	3	2	2	1

당신이 방에 틀어 박혀 있다고 상상해 보자. 슬퍼하지 말라

You'll slip on a virtual reality (VR) helmet and enjoy a virtual party with your friends

S	V	O2		conj	V	O1	ad.p
1	3	2		4	8	7	6

on a computer.

ad.p
5

당신은 가상 현실 헬멧을 쓰고 컴퓨터상에서 당신의 친구들과 가상 파티를 즐기게 될 것이다.

You might use a VR helmet to play along inside a television game show, join your favorite rock

s	v	o1	ad.p	ad.p	(to) ad.p	O1'
1	11	10	3	2	6	5

band onstage, or leap into an action ,film

	ad	conj	ad.p	ad.p
	4	7	9	8

당신은 텔레비전 게임쇼 안에 들어가 게임을 하거나 무대 위에서 당신의 좋아하는 밴드와 함께하거나 액션 영화에 출연하기 위해 가상 현실 헬멧을 쓸지 모른다.

The future will be bright for couch potatoes!

     S   V   C2   ad.p

     1   4   3   2

미래가 소파족(Couch potatoes)들에게 밝을 것이다.

DOOR-TO-DOOR DRIVERLESS TAXIS

운전자 없이 집집마다 데려다 주는 택시

(Is there) No cars in the future? No problem!

    V   S   ad.p

    3   2   1

미래에 차가 없다고? 문제 없어요

At a taxi station, you'll simply say your destination into a voice-recognition machine.

ad.p   S   ad   V   O1   ad.p

1   2   5   6   4   3

당신은 음성 인식 기계에다 당신의 목적지를 간단히 말하면 될 것이다.

A door will open to a small, automated taxi as the fare is (electronically)paid from your bank

 S   V   ad.p   ad.c   S   ad   V

 6   8   7   5   1   3   4

account..

    ad.p

     2

요금이 당신의 은행계좌로부터 자동적으로 지불되면서 문이 작고 자동화된 택시에 열릴 것이다.

Then the taxi will take you to your destination.

   ad S   V   O1   ad.p

   1   2   5   4   3

그런 다음 그 택시가 당신의 목적지까지 당신을 데려다 줄 것이다.

MIRACLE CHIPS

기적의 칩

"Billy? 빌리?
Where are you?"
   ad   V   S
    3   2   1
어디에 있니?

When a child gets lost, the parents will find him or her without difficulty.
ad.c   S   V C2   S   V   O1   ad.p
4   1   3 2   5   8   7   6
아이를 잃어 버렸을 때, 그 부모는 어려움 없이 아이를 찾게 될 것이다.

Every child will carry a microchip, and it will help the parents to find them.
   S   V   O1   conj S   V   O   C3 O1'
   1   3   2   4 5   9   6   8   7
모든 아이들이 마이크로 칩을 지니고 다닐 것이고, 그것이 (마이크로칩) 그 부모가 아이들을 찾도록 도울 것이다.

The same kind of chip could (also) serve as a library card, driver's license, and medical record.
      S   V   ad   ad.p
      1   4   3   2
같은 종류의 칩이 도서관 카드, 운전면허증, 의료카드로서 역시 사용될 것이다.

Wonders in the future are probably beyond our imagination.
   S   a.p   V   ad   ad.p
   2   1   5   3   4
미래의 경이로움은 아마도 우리의 상상 너머에 있을 것이다. (놀라울 것이다.)

"We study the future so (that) we can prepare for tomorrow," explains Joseph Coates, a futurist

S	V	O1	ad.c	S	V	ad.p	v	s	(동격)
1	7	6	5	2	4	3	10	9	

from Washington, D.C.

a.p

8

우리는 미래에 대하여 준비하기 위하여 미래를 연구한다고 워싱턴 DC 출신의 미래연구가인 조셉 코우츠가 설명한다.

Futurists help companies and governments plan ahead – but not too far ahead.

S	V	O1	C4	ad	conj	ad
1	5	2	4	3	6	7

미래연구가들은 회사와 정부가 미리(앞서서) 계획세우는 것을 돕지만 – 너무 앞서지는 않는다.

Technology is changing quickly, so predictions that look beyond the next 30 years would be

S	v	ad	ad	S	a.c	V1	ad.p	V2
1	3	2	4	7	6		5	10

mostly guesswork

ad	C1
8	9

과학 기술은 빨리 변화하고 있다. 그래서 향후 30년을 넘어서서 전망하는 예언은 거의 추측이 될 것이다.

"Looking into the future is an art, not a science" says Coates.

S	O2'	V	C1	V	S
2	1	4	3	6	5

"미래를 연구한다는 것은 예술이지 과학이 아니다."라고 코우츠는 말한다.

Bomba Escapes from the Zoo

When you are writing, ask yourself (what your purpose is.)

ad,c	S	V	V	O7	O7	S	V
3	1	2	8	4	7	5	6

당신이 글을 쓸 때 당신 자신에게 당신의 목적이 되는 것을 물어 보라.

Are you writing simply to express your own feelings?

S	V	ad	ad,p	o1'
1	5	2	4	3

당신은 단지 당신 자신의 감정을 표현하기 위해 글을 쓰고 있는가?

Are you writing to give facts and other kinds of information?

S	V	ad,p	O1'
1	4	3	2

당신은 사실과 다른 종류의 정보들을 주기 위해 글을 쓰고 있는가?

Are you writing to persuade other people to change their minds about something?

S	V	a,d,p	o'	c3'	O1'	ad,p
1	7	6	2	5	4	3

당신은 다른 사람들이 무엇인가에 관하여 그들의 마음을 변화시키도록 설득하기 위해 글을 쓰고 있는가?

The writings that follow are about the same subject.

S	V1	V2	ad,p
2	1	4	3

다음 글들은 같은 주제에 관한 것이다.

But each has a different purpose .

conj	S	V	O1
1	2	4	3

그러나 각각의 글들은 다른 목적이 있다.

As you read, think about how differently the subject is presented for each purpose.

ad.c s   v   v   ad   S   v   ad.p

3   1   2   8   5   4   7   6

당신이 읽으면서, 그 주제가 얼마나 다르게 각각의 목적에 따라 제시되었는가를 생각해 보라.

[1]

I will never forget the first time that (I saw Bomba the monkey at the Evanstown Zoo).

S   V   O1   a.c S   V   O1   ad.p

1   7   6   2   5   4   3

나는 내가 에반스를 동물원에서 원숭이 봄바를 본 처음 시간을 결코 잊을 수 없을 것이다.

It was a sunny Sunday afternoon.

S   V   c1

2   1

어느 화창한 일요일 오후였다.

The place was packed with people watching the new monkey.

S   V   ad.p   a.p   O1'

1   5   4   3   2

그 곳은 그 새 원숭이를 구경하는 사람들로 붐비고 있었다.

I felt (that) Bomba was doing all of his tricks just for me.

S V   O6   S   V   O1   ad.p

1 6   2   5   4   3

나는 봄바가 오직 나마을 위해 온갖 그의 재주를 부리고 있다고 느꼈다.

If I waved at him, he waved at me. If I scratched my head, he scratched his head.

ad.c S v   ad.p S   V   ad.p ad.c S v   o1   S   V   O1

4   1 3   2   5   7   6   4   1 3   2   5   7   6

내가 그에게 손을 흔들었을 때 그가 내게 손을 흔들었다. 내가 내 머리를 긁적였을 때 그가 자기의 머리를 긁적였다.

An old man standing by me said, "Well, this monkey sure likes you!"

S		a,p	ad,p	V	ad		S	ad	V	O1
3		2	1	4	5		6	8	9	7

내 옆에 있던 노인이 말했다. "음, 이 원숭이는 당신을 정말 좋아하고 있군요.!"

I never did go to see the zookeepers giving the baby elephant a bath.

S	ad	V	ad,p	O'	C5'	O7	O'7
1	7	8	6	2	5	3	4

나는 동물원 사육사가 아기 코끼리에게 목욕시키는 것을 보기 위해 결코 가지 않았다.

Instead, I stayed by the monkey cage for two or three hours

ad	S	V	ad,p	ad,p
1	2	5	4	3

대신에 나는 두세 시간 동안 원숭이가 우리 곁에 머물러 있었다.

I felt sad to leave Bomba, and he seemed sorry to see me go

S	V	C2	ad,p	O1'	conj	S	V	C2	ad,p	O	C4'
1	5	4	3	2		6	7	12	11	10	8	9

나는 봄바를 떠나게 돼서 슬펐고, 그는 내가 가게 되어서 슬픈 듯이 보였다.

I promised him (that) I'd be back soon.

S	V	O7	S	V	ad
1	6	5	2	4	3

나는 곧 돌아오겠다고 그에게 약속했다.

Then I got busy with school work, soccer, and all kinds of other things.

ad	S	V	C2	ad,p
1	2	5	4	3

그 후 나는 숙제, 운동, 모든 종류의 다른 일들로 바빴다.

I was planning to go to see Bomba again this weekend.

S	V	O3	ad,p	o1'	ad	ad
1	7	6	5	4	3	2

나는 이번 주 다시 봄바를 보기 위해 가기로 마음먹고 있었다.

But now an article in the newspaper says that (Bomba escape Yesterday).

conj	ad	S	a,p	V	O6	S	v	ad
1	2	4	3	8		5	7	6

그러나 지금 신문에 있는 기사가 봄바가 어제 탈출했다고 보도한다.

There's a big reward for giving information about Bomba.   I don't want any money.

V	S	a,p	O1'	ad,p	S	V	O1'
5	4	3	2	1	1	3	2

봄바에 대해 정보를 제공하는 데 대한 큰 보상이 있다..   나는 어떠한 돈도 원치 않는다.

I just want Bomba to be back safely in his cage.

s	ad	V	O	C3	ad	ad,p
2	1	7	3	6	5	4

단지 나는 봄바가 그의 우리에 안전하게 돌아오기를 원한다.

[2]
MONKEY ESCAPES FROM ZOO

원숭이가 동물원에서 탈출하다.

A monkey escaped from the Evanstown Zoo yesterday.

S	V	ad,p	ad
1	4	3	2

한 원숭이가 어제 에반스톤 동물원에서 탈출했다.

Zoo officials are offering a $1,000 reward for information.

S	V	O1	ad.p
1	4	3	2

동물원 관리자들은 정보에 대해 1000달러의 보상을 줄 것이다.

The spider monkey, known as Bomba, is brown and weighs ten pounds nine ounces.

S	a.p	ad.p	V	C2	conj	V	o1
3	2	1	5	4	6	8	7

봄바로 알려진 거미 원숭이는 갈색이고 10파운드 9온스가 나간다.

It was born in the zoo and has(always) lived there.

S	V	ad.p	conj	V	ad
1	3	2	4	6	5

그것은(the spider monkey) 동물원에서 태어났고 늘 거기서 살아 왔다.

Andrea Coleman, Director of the Zoo, asks the public not to try to capture the monkey.

S	(동격)	V	O	C3	O5′	O1′
2	1	7	3	6	5	4

동물원 원장인 안드레아 콜맨은 일반인들이 그 원숭이를 잡지 않기를 요청한다.

For the safety of the public and the monkey, special animal handlers will be available 24 hours

ad.p	a.p	s	v	c2	ad
2	1	3	6	5	4

a day.

ad

일반인들과 원숭이의 안전을 위하여 동물 특별 조련사들이 하루 24시간 이용가능하다. (항상 대기하고 있다.)

Anyone having any information about the missing monkey is asked to call Ms. Coleman at the

	S	a.p	O1'		a.p	V	o3	O1'
	3	4	2		1	8	7	6

special Missing Animals Hot Line,555-ZOOS.

	ad.p
	5

잃어버린 원숭이에 관한 어떠한 정보라도 가진 사람들은 특설전화 MAHL 555-2005로 미즈 코울맨에게 전화를 걸도록 요청된다.(전화해 주세요.)

[3]
Dear Town Councilman Smith:

시의원 스미스씨께

The escape of Bomba the monkey from the Evanstown Zoo reminds us (that we need more

	S	a.p	a.p	V	O7	O7	S	V
	3	2	1	9	4		5	8

guards at the zoo).

O1	ad.p
7	6

Because of cuts in funding, the number of zoo guards has been cut in half.

	ad.p	a.p	S	a.p	V	ad.p
	2	1	4	3	6	5

에반스톤동물원부터의 봄바 원숭이의 탈출은 우리가 동물원에서 더 많은 경비원들을 필요로 한다는 사실을 우리에게 일깨워 주었다. 자금의 삭감 때문에 동물원 경비원의 수가 절반으로 줄었다.

Instead of two guards patrolling the zoo grounds, there is now only one.

	ad.p	a.p	O1'	V	ad	S
	3	2	1	6	4	5

동물원 경내를 순찰하는 두 명의 경비원 대신에 지금 단 한 명만이 있다.

There are two reasons to keep two guards on duty at all times.

V	S	a.p	o1'	ad.p	ad.p
6	5	4	3	2	1

항상 근무를 서는 두 명의 경비를 유지하는 두 가지 이유가 있다.

The first reason is for the safety and protection of animals in the zoo.

S	V	ad.p	a.p	a.p
1	5	4	3	2

그 첫째 이유는 동물원에 있는 동물의 안전과 보호를 위해서이다.

The second reason is for the safety and protection of the public.

S	V	ad.p	a.p
1	4	3	2

두 번째 이유는 일반인의 안전과 보호를 위한 것이다.

I urge you to vote "yes" on the bill (that will provide more funding for the zoo.)

S	v	o	C3	O1'	ad.p	a.c	V	O1	ad.p
1	9	2	8	7	6		5	4	3

나는 당신이 동물원을 위해 더 많은 자금을 제공하게 될 법안에 찬성표를 던질 것을 권한다.

〈수능기출 1번〉

Growing as a person may take you to new places and present new challenges.

S	ad.p	V	O1	ad.p	conj	V	O1
2	1	5	4	3	6	8	7

한 사람으로서 성장한다는 것은 새로운 곳으로 당신을 데려가서(이끌어서) 새로운 도전을 제공하게 될지도 모른다.

These may be stressful, but feeling stress is a natural, necessary part of recognizing a weakness

These	may	be	stressful,	but	feeling	stress	is	a natural, necessary part		of	recognizing a weakness
S	v		C2	conj	S	O1′	V	C1		a.p	O1′
1	2		3	4	6	5	13	12		8	7

and trying out a new behavior.

and	trying out	a new behavior.
conj	a.p	O1
9	11	10

이것들은 스트레스가 많을진 몰라도(but) 스트레스를 느낀다는 것은 연약함을 깨닫고 새로운 행동을 만들어 내는 데 자연스럽고 필수적인 부분이다.

It is often comfortable and easy to stay the way (that) we are.

It	is	often	comfortable and easy	to stay	the way	(that)	we	are.
	V	ad	C2	S	ad.p	a.c	S	V
	7	5	6	4	3		1	2

우리가 있는 방식대로(하던 대로) 머물러 있다는 것은 종종 편하고 쉽다.

Giving up old comforts and habits is very hard.

Giving up	old comforts and habits	is	very	hard.
s	o2′	v	ad	c2
2	1	5	3	4

오랜 안락함과 습관들을 포기한다는 것은 대단히 힘들다.

It is small wonder, then (that people dislike changing).

It	is	small wonder,	then	(that	people	dislike	changing).
	v	C1	ad		S	V	O4
	6	5	4		1	3	2

사람들이 변화하기를 싫어하는 것은 게다가 작은 놀라움이다. (놀랄 일이 아니다.)

〈수능기출 2번〉

Since the mid-1990s, teaching Korean to foreigners has made quiet and steady progress.

Since the mid-1990s,	teaching	Korean	to foreigners	has made	quiet and steady progress.
ad.p	S	O1′	ad.p	V	O1
1	4	3	2	6	5

1990 년대 중반 래, 외국인에게 한국어를 가르치는 것은 조용하고도 꾸준한 진보를 이루어 왔다.

Many Universities now offer Korean language programs in Korea and aboard, and many

S   ad   V   O1   ad.p   conj   S

2   1   5   4   3   6   7

textbooks have been produced for learners of Korean

V   ad.p   a.p

10   9   8

이제 많은 대학들이 한국과 해외에서 한국어 프로그램을 제공하고 있고 많은 교과서들이 한국어 학습자를 위해 만들어졌다.

(Only) a small number of foreigners, however, have benefited form this progress.

s   ad   v   ad.p

2   1   4   3

그러나 소수의 외국인들만이 이런 발전으로부터 혜택을 받았다.

Most foreign workers are being taught by Korean coworkers or volunteers (who have no or little

S   v   ad.p   a.c   v

1   5   4   3

teaching experience.)

o1

2

대부분의 외국인 노동자들이 가르치는 경험이 없거나 약간 있는 동료나 자원봉사자들에 의해 가르침을 받고 있다.

Thus, it is necessary to establish better educational programs for teaching the Korean language

Ad   v   c2   s   o1'   a.p   o1'

1   8   7   6   5   4   3

to foreign workers.

ad.p

2

그러므로 외국 노동자들에게 한국어를 가르치기 위한 더 나은 교육 프로그램을 수립하는 것은 필요하다.

〈 수능기출 3번〉

There was a kind woman who made a last attempt to catch up.
  V1   s   a.c   v2   O1   a.p
  6   5   4   3   2   1

잡으려는 마지막 시도를 한 친절한 여인이 있었다.

Seeing a box of 50 identical greeting cards in a shop, she snapped (it) up,
 ad.p   O'   ad.p   S   V   (O2)
  3   2   1   4   6   5

c rried it home, and signed 49 cards before midnight.
  V O1 ad conj   V   O1   ad.p
  9   8   7   10   13   12   11

가게에서 50개의 동일한 카드 한 상자를 본 그 여자는 그것을 덥석 집어서 집으로 그것을 가져 왔고 자정전에 49개의 카드에 서명했다.

She posted them the next morning and gave a sigh of relief.
 S   V   O1   ad.p   conj   v   o1   a.p
 1   4   3   2   5   8   7   6

그 여자는 그 다음날 그것들을 부치고서 안도의 숨을 쉬었다.

Then she opened one remaining card, and found these words printed on it:
 Ad   s   V   O1   conj   V   O1   a.p   ad.p
  1   2   4   3   5   9   8   7   6

그런 다음 그 여자는 남아 있는 한 장의 카드를 열었는데 이런 말들이 그 위에 씌어진 것을 알게 되었다.

:This little card is just to say that a gift from me is on the way.)
       S   V ad C4   (O6') S   ad.p   V   ad.p
       1   8   6   7   3   2   5   4

이 작은 카드는 단지 저로부터의 선물(제가 보낸)이 가고 있는 중이라는 사실을 알리려는 것뿐이다.

〈수능기출 4번〉

Thomas Jefferson once said (that what matters is the courage of one's convictions.)
      S   ad   V O6   S   V   C1   a.p 2
      2   1   7   3   6   5   4

한때 토마스 제퍼슨은 중요한 것은 자신의 신념에 대한 용기라는 것을 말했다.

Do you have the courage(which comes from the sincere conviction that you are a person of
   S V   O1   a.c   V   ad.p   S   V   C1   a.p
   1 10   9   8   7   2   6   5   4

sound character, an honest, dependable, kind, and caring person?
                        C1
                        3

당신은 당신이 건전한 인격의 사람이고 정직하고 신뢰할 만하고 친절하며 봉사적인 사람이라는 진지한 확신에서 나온 용기를 지니고 있는가?

If you do, you will never have to worry about what others think of you.
ad.c S V S   V   ad.p   s   v   o2
3 1 2 4   9   8   5   7   6

당신이 그렇다면, 당신은 다른 사람들이 어떻게 당신을 생각할까에 대하여 결코 걱정할 필요가 없을 것이다.

If you know in your heart that you are a good and decent person, you can meet life's
ad.c s v   ad.p   O6 s v   c1   s   v   o
7 1 6   5   2 4   3   8   15   14

challenges head-on and without fear of what others think.
             ad   conj   ad.p   a.p s   v
             9   13   11   10 12

만약 당신이 선량하고 괜찮은 사람이라는 사실을 마음속에 알고 있다면, 당신은 정면으로 그리고 다른 사람들이 어떻게 생각하는가에 대한 두려움 없이 삶의 도전을 대처할 수 있다.

A terrible accident changed my life. A friend and I were driving home from a mid night
      S   V   O1   S   V   ad   ad,p
      1   3   2   1   4   3   2

movie.
끔찍한 사고가 내 인생을 바꿨다. 한 친구와 내가 심야 영화를 본 후 집으로 운전하며 가고 있었다.

As we approached an intersection, we stopped at a red light.
ad.c S   V   O1   S   V   ad,p
 4   1   3   2   5   7   6
우리가 교차로에 접근하면서, 우리는 빨간불에 멈춰섰다.

No cars seemed to be coming, so I decided to go through the red light. Immediately after
    s   v   conj s   v   o3   ad,p   ad.c
    1   2   3 4   7   6   5   3

we started, I lost consciousness.
 s   v   s   v   o1
 1   2   4   6   5
아무런 차도 오는 것 같지 않아서, 나는 빨간불을 지나쳐 가기로 결정했다. 우리가 출발한 후 곧바로, 나는 의식을 잃었다.

Later I learned that we had hit a car coming from the other direction.)
 ad s   v   o6   s   v   o1   a,p   ad,p
 1   2   8   3   7   6   5   4
후에 나는 우리가 다른 방향에서 달려오는 차와 부딪쳤다는 것을 알았다.

That accident made my friend spend the rest of his life in a wheelchair, and I learned a costly
     S   v   o   c4   o1'   a,p   a,p   conj s   v   o1
     1   7   2   6   5   4   3   8 9   11   10

lesson.
그 사고로 나의 친구는 휠체어에서 그의 나머지 평생을 보내게 되었고 나는 값비싼 교훈을 배웠다.

고급문장

1. As the tadpole grows older, the cells composing its tail are attacked and absorbed by certain
   ad.c   S   V   older,   S   composing O1'   V   ad.p
   4   1   3   2   14   13   12   16   15

   body cells until the tail shrinks and (finally) diasppears completely.
              ad.c   S   V   conj   ad   V   ad
              11   5   6   7   8   10   9

올챙이가 점점 나이 먹어감에 따라 그 꼬리가 움츠러들고 마침내 완전히 사라질 때까지 그것의(올챙이의) 꼬리를 구성하는
세포들이 어떤 몸세포들에 의해 공격받고 흡수된다

2. During the American Revolution the people of Canada remained loyal to England although
   ad.p   S   a.p   V   C2   ad.p   ad.c
   1   11   10   14   13   12   9

   the rebelling colonies tried to persuade them to join the war for indendence.
   S   V   O5   O'   C3'   O1'   a.p
   2   8   7   3   6   5   4

미국 혁명 동안에 저항하는 식민지들은 그들로(캐나다국민) 독립을 위한 전쟁에 참여하도록 설득하려 했지만 캐나다 국민들
은 영국에 충성을 계속하였다.

3. The Korean economic system does not exist in isolation but is a part of the world-wide
   S   V   ad.p   conj V C1   a.p
   1   3   2   4   7 6   5

   economic system.

   Thus, the economic life of the Korean people is greatly affectted by the
   ad   S   a.p   ad   V   ad.p
   1   3   2   6   7   5

   economic life of all the peoples.
                   a.p
                   4

한국 경제 체계는 고립하여 존재하지 않고 전 세계 경제 체제의 일부분이다. 그래서 한국민의 경제 생활은
모든 국가 국민들의 경제 생활에 의해 크게 영향받고 있다.

4. Today, our enourmous investment in science and research is the evidence of our faith (that
     ad   S   a.p   V   C1   a.p   동격절
     1   3   2   14   13   12

   science can not only make man richer but it can make man better.)
     S   V   O   C2   S   V   O   C2
     4   7   5   6   8   11   9   10

   그 오늘날 과학과 연구에 대한 우리의 엄청난 투자는 과학이 사람을 더욱 부하게 할 수 있을 뿐 아니라 그것이 사람을 더 낫게 할 수 있다는 믿음의 증거이다.

   not only A but (also) B = A할 뿐만 아니라 B하다.

5. But in 1799 an officer in Napoleon's army discovered (near the Egyptian village of Rpsetta)
   conj   ad.p   S   a.p   V   ad.p
    1   2   4   3   11   10

   a smooth, thick black stone covered with carvings(that were divided into three separate
              O1   a.p   ad.p   a,c   v   ad.p
              9   8   7   6   5

   secttions.)

   그러나 1799년에 나폴레옹군의 한 장교가 세 개의 별개의 부분으로 나뉘어 있는 새긴 비문들로 덮여 있는 부드럽고 두꺼운 검정색돌을 로제타라는 이집트 마을 근처에서 발견했다.

6. In northern countries many insects and worms that cannot live in winter) die when cold
         ad.p   S   a.c   V1   ad.p   V2   ad.c   S
         4   7   6   5   8   3   1

   weather comes. They leave larvae, or egg, to revive their species the following spring.
         V   S   V   O1   ad.p   O1'   ad.p
         2   1   6   5   4   3   2

   추운 날씨가 되면, 북쪽 나라에서는 겨울에 살 수 없는 많은 곤충과 벌레들이 죽는다. 그들이 그 다음해에 그들의 종을 소생시키기 위해 유충 혹은 알을 남겨 놓는다.

7. The animal's mouth is disproportionately large in comparison with his narrow throat. When

	S	V	ad	C2	ad.p	ad.p	ad.c
	1	6	4	5	3	2	5

he fills his mouth with food, he must chew for a long time before he can swallow.

S	V	O1	ad.p	S	V	ad.p	ad.c	S	V
1	4	3	2	9	11	10	8	6	7

동물들의 입은 좁은 입과 비교해서 어울리지 않게 크다. 그(동물)가 음식으로 그의 입을 채울 때 그가 삼킬 수 있기 전에 그는 오랫동안 반드시 씹어야 한다. (그가 오랫동안 씹어야만 삼킬 수 있다.)

8. If democracy is to survive, above all the thing (that a teacher should endeavor to produce in

ad.c	S	V	ad.p	S	a.c	S	V	O3	ad.p
3	1	2	4	9		5	8	7	6

his pupils) is the kind of tolerance (that springs from an endeavor to understand those (who are

	V	C1	a.p	a.c	V	ad.c	a.p	O1'	a.c	V
	19	18	17		16	15	14	13		12

different from ourselves.)

	C1	ad.p
	11	10

민주주의가 살아남으려 한다면, 무엇보다도 선생님이 그의 학생들 안에 만들어 내기를 노력해야 하는 것은 우리 자신들과 다른 사람들을 이해하는 노력으로부터 나오는 관용의 방식이다.

9. Just when many of the nation's contractors were looking into moving out of the industry,

	ad.c	S	a.p	V	O2	ad.p
	6	2	1	5	4	3

the unfortunate result of the earthquake has created an enourmous demand for construction.

S	a.p	V	O1	a.p
8	7	11	10	9

국내의 토건업자들 중 다수가 사업에서 손을 떼려고 고민하고 있을 바로 그때, 지진이라는 불행한 결과가 건축에 대한 막대한 수요를 창출해냈다.

10. Drama thrived in India a long time ago, and since the plays presented there always had

S	V	ad.p	ad		conj	ad.c	S		a.p	ad	ad	V
1	4	3	2		5	12	8		7	6	9	11

happy endings, Hindu theatergoers were strangers to tragedies.

O1	S	V	O2
10	13	15	14

연극이 오래 전에 인도에서 번성했는데 거기에서 상연된 연극들이 항상 행복한 결말로 끝났기 때문에, 인도 관객들은 비극을 몰랐다.

MEMO

MEMO

MEMO